MznLnx

Missing Links Exam Preps

Exam Prep for

Essentials of Entrepreneurship and Small Business Management

Zimmerer, Scarborough, 4th Edition

The MznLnx Exam Prep is your link from the texbook and lecture to your exams.
The MznLnx Exam Preps are unauthorized and comprehensive reviews of your textbooks.

All material provided by MznLnx and Rico Publications (c) 2010
Textbook publishers and textbook authors do not particpate in or contribute to these reviews.

MznLnx

Rico
Publications

Exam Prep for Essentials of Entrepreneurship and Small Business Management
4th Edition
Zimmerer, Scarborough

Publisher: Raymond Houge
Assistant Editor: Michael Rouger
Text and Cover Designer: Lisa Buckner
Marketing Manager: Sara Swagger
Project Manager, Editorial Production: Jerry Emerson
Art Director: Vernon Lowerui

Product Manager: Dave Mason
Editorial Assitant: Rachel Guzmanji
Pedagogy: Debra Long
Cover Image: Jim Reed/Getty Images
Text and Cover Printer: City Printing, Inc.
Compositor: Media Mix, Inc.

(c) 2010 Rico Publications
ALL RIGHTS RESERVED. No part of this work
covered by the copyright may be reproduced or
used in any form or by an means--graphic, electronic,
or mechanical, including photocopying, recording,
taping, Web distribution, information storage, and
retrieval systems, or in any other manner--without the
written permission of the publisher.

Printed in the United States
ISBN:

For more information about our products, contact us at:
Dave.Mason@RicoPublications.com

For permission to use material from this text or
product, submit a request online to:
Dave.Mason@RicoPublications.com

Contents

CHAPTER 1
The Foundations of Entrepreneurship — 1

CHAPTER 2
Inside the Entrepreneurial Mind: From Ideas to Reality — 8

CHAPTER 3
Strategic Management and the Entrepreneur — 11

CHAPTER 4
Forms of Business Ownership and Franchising — 16

CHAPTER 5
Buying an Existing Business — 24

CHAPTER 6
Building a Powerful Marketing Plan — 29

CHAPTER 7
E-Commerce and the Entrepreneur — 39

CHAPTER 8
Integrated Marketing Communications and Pricing Strategies — 44

CHAPTER 9
Managing Cash Flow — 52

CHAPTER 10
Creating a Successful Financial Plan — 57

CHAPTER 11
Crafting a Winning Business Plan — 66

CHAPTER 12
Sources of Financing: Debt and Equity — 73

CHAPTER 13
Choosing the Right Location and Layout — 81

CHAPTER 14
Global Aspects of Entrepreneurship — 85

CHAPTER 15
Leading the Growing Company and Planning for Management Succession — 90

ANSWER KEY — 102

TO THE STUDENT

COMPREHENSIVE

The *MznLnx* Exam Prep series is designed to help you pass your exams. Editors at MznLnx review your textbooks and then prepare these practice exams to help you master the textbook material. Unlike study guides, workbooks, and practice tests provided by the texbook publisher and textbook authors, *MznLnx* gives you **all** of the material in each chapter in exam form, not just samples, so you can be sure to nail your exam.

MECHANICAL

The MznLnx Exam Prep series creates exams that will help you learn the subject matter as well as test you on your understanding. Each question is designed to help you master the concept. Just working through the exams, you gain an understanding of the subject--its a simple mechanical process that produces success.

INTEGRATED STUDY GUIDE AND REVIEW

MznLnx is not just a set of exams designed to test you, its also a comprehensive review of the subject content. Each exam question is also a review of the concept, making sure that you will get the answer correct without having to go to other sources of material. You learn as you go! Its the easiest way to pass an exam.

HUMOR

Studying can be tedious and dry. MznLnx's instructional design includes moderate humor within the exam questions on occassion, to break the tedium and revitalize the brain

Chapter 1. The Foundations of Entrepreneurship 1

1. An _____ is a person who has possession of an enterprise and assumes significant accountability for the inherent risks and the outcome. It is an ambitious leader who combines land, labor, and capital to create and market new goods or services. The term is a loanword from French and was first defined by the Irish economist Richard Cantillon.
   a. AAAI
   b. A4e
   c. A Stake in the Outcome
   d. Entrepreneur

2. _____, commonly abbreviated to Gen X, is a term used to refer to a generational cohort of children born after the baby boom ended and usually prior to the 1980s

   The term _____ has been used in demography, the social sciences, and marketing, though it is most often used in popular culture.

   In the U.S. _____ was originally referred to as the 'baby bust' generation because of the drop in the birth rate following the baby boom.

   a. Adam Smith
   b. Affiliation
   c. Abraham Harold Maslow
   d. Generation X

3. _____ is a term used to describe the demographic cohort following Generation X. Its members are often referred to as 'Millennials' or 'Echo Boomers') . There are no precise dates for when Gen Y begins and ends. Most commentators use dates from the early 1980s to early 1990s.
   a. David Wittig
   b. Generation Y
   c. Giovanni Agnelli
   d. Benjamin R. Barber

4. A _____ is a business that is privately owned and operated, with a small number of employees and relatively low volume of sales. The legal definition of 'small' often varies by country and industry, but is generally under 100 employees in the United States and under 50 employees in the European Union. In comparison, the definition of mid-sized business by the number of employees is generally under 500 in the U.S. and 250 for the European Union.
   a. Golden Boot Compensation
   b. Pre-determined overhead rate
   c. Small business
   d. Critical Success Factor

5. The term '_____' refers to the concept of collecting information and attempting to spot a pattern in the information. In some fields of study, the term '_____' has more formally-defined meanings.

   In project management _____ is a mathematical technique that uses historical results to predict future outcome.

   a. Regression analysis
   b. Trend analysis
   c. Stepwise regression
   d. Least squares

6. _____ describes the situation when output from (or information about the result of) an event or phenomenon in the past will influence the same event/phenomenon in the present or future. When an event is part of a chain of cause-and-effect that forms a circuit or loop, then the event is said to 'feed back' into itself.

_____ is also a synonym for:

- _____ signal; the information about the initial event that is the basis for subsequent modification of the event.
- _____ loop; the causal path that leads from the initial generation of the _____ signal to the subsequent modification of the event.

_____ is a mechanism, process or signal that is looped back to control a system within itself. Such a loop is called a _____ loop.

a. 1990 Clean Air Act
c. Feedback loop
b. Positive feedback
d. Feedback

7. In decision theory and estimation theory, the _____ of an estimator, $\hat{\theta}$, of an unknown parameter of the distribution, θ, is the expected value of the loss function

$$R(\theta, \hat{\theta}) = \mathbb{E}_\theta L(\theta, \hat{\theta}) = \int L(\theta, \hat{\theta})\, dP_\theta.$$

where dP_θ is a probability measure parametrized by θ.

- For a scalar parameter θ and a quadratic loss function,

$$L(\theta, \hat{\theta}) = (\theta - \hat{\theta})^2$$

  the _____ function becomes the mean squared error of the estimate,

$$R(\theta, \hat{\theta}) = E_\theta (\theta - \hat{\theta})^2$$

- In density estimation, the unknown parameter is probability density itself. The loss function is typically chosen to be a norm in an appropriate function space. For example, for L^2 norm,

$$L(f, \hat{f}) = \|f - \hat{f}\|_2^2$$

  the _____ function becomes the mean integrated squared error

$$R(f, \hat{f}) = E\|f - \hat{f}\|^2$$

a. Financial modeling
b. Risk
c. Risk aversion
d. Linear model

8. _____ according to Onuoha (2007) is the practice of starting new organizations or revitalizing mature organizations, particularly new businesses generally in response to identified opportunities. _____ is often a difficult undertaking, as a vast majority of new businesses fail. Entrepreneurial activities are substantially different depending on the type of organization that is being started.
   a. A Stake in the Outcome
   b. Entrepreneurship
   c. AAAI
   d. A4e

9. The 'business case for _____', theorizes that in a global marketplace, a company that employs a diverse workforce (both men and women, people of many generations, people from ethnically and racially diverse backgrounds etc.) is better able to understand the demographics of the marketplace it serves and is thus better equipped to thrive in that marketplace than a company that has a more limited range of employee demographics.

An additional corollary suggests that a company that supports the _____ of its workforce can also improve employee satisfaction, productivity and retention.

   a. Virtual team
   b. Trademark
   c. Kanban
   d. Diversity

10. Engineering _____ is the permissible limit of variation in

    1. a physical dimension,
    2. a measured value or physical property of a material, manufactured object, system, or service,
    3. other measured values (such as temperature, humidity, etc.)
    4. in engineering and safety, a physical distance or space (_____), as in a truck (lorry), train or boat under a bridge as well as a train in a tunnel

Dimensions, properties, or conditions may vary within certain practical limits without significantly affecting functioning of equipment or a process. _____s are specified to allow reasonable leeway for imperfections and inherent variability without compromising performance.

The _____ may be specified as a factor or percentage of the nominal value, a maximum deviation from a nominal value, an explicit range of allowed values, be specified by a note or published standard with this information, or be implied by the numeric accuracy of the nominal value. _____ can be symmetrical, as in 40±0.1, or asymmetrical, such as 40+0.2/−0.1.

   a. Quality assurance
   b. Zero defects
   c. Root cause analysis
   d. Tolerance

11. The _____ captures an expanded spectrum of values and criteria for measuring organizational success: economic, ecological and social. With the ratification of the United Nations and ICLEI _____ standard for urban and community accounting in early 2007, this became the dominant approach to public sector full cost accounting. Similar UN standards apply to natural capital and human capital measurement to assist in measurements required by _____, e.g. the ecoBudget standard for reporting ecological footprint.

a. 33 Strategies of War
c. 28-hour day
b. Triple bottom line
d. 1990 Clean Air Act

12. The _____ or gross domestic income (GDI), a basic measure of an economy's economic performance, is the market value of all final goods and services made within the borders of a nation in a year. _____ can be defined in three ways, all of which are conceptually identical. First, it is equal to the total expenditures for all final goods and services produced within the country in a stipulated period of time (usually a 365-day year).
  a. Perfect competition
  c. Human capital
  b. Productivity management
  d. Gross domestic product

13. _____ is a financial metric which represents operating liquidity available to a business. Along with fixed assets such as plant and equipment, _____ is considered a part of operating capital. It is calculated as current assets minus current liabilities.
  a. 33 Strategies of War
  c. Working Capital
  b. 1990 Clean Air Act
  d. 28-hour day

14. _____ is a mathematical science pertaining to the collection, analysis, interpretation or explanation, and presentation of data. It also provides tools for prediction and forecasting based on data. It is applicable to a wide variety of academic disciplines, from the natural and social sciences to the humanities, government and business.
  a. Statistics
  c. Failure rate
  b. Location parameter
  d. Simple moving average

15. _____ or _____ data refers to selected population characteristics as used in government, marketing or opinion research, or the _____ profiles used in such research. Note the distinction from the term 'demography' Commonly-used _____s include race, age, income, disabilities, mobility (in terms of travel time to work or number of vehicles available), educational attainment, home ownership, employment status, and even location.
  a. Adam Smith
  c. Abraham Harold Maslow
  b. Demographic
  d. Affiliation

16. _____ is an advertisement in which a particular product specifically mentions a competitor by name for the express purpose of showing why the competitor is inferior to the product naming it.

This should not be confused with parody advertisements, where a fictional product is being advertised for the purpose of poking fun at the particular advertisement, nor should it be confused with the use of a coined brand name for the purpose of comparing the product without actually naming an actual competitor. ('Wikipedia tastes better and is less filling than the Encyclopedia Galactica.')

In the 1980s, during what has been referred to as the cola wars, soft-drink manufacturer Pepsi ran a series of advertisements where people, caught on hidden camera, in a blind taste test, chose Pepsi over rival Coca-Cola.

  a. 33 Strategies of War
  c. 1990 Clean Air Act
  b. 28-hour day
  d. Comparative advertising

17. _____ is an integrated communications-based process through which individuals and communities discover that existing and newly-identified needs and wants may be satisfied by the products and services of others.

Chapter 1. The Foundations of Entrepreneurship

_____ is defined by the American _____ Association as the activity, set of institutions, and processes for creating, communicating, delivering, and exchanging offerings that have value for customers, clients, partners, and society at large. The term developed from the original meaning which referred literally to going to market, as in shopping, or going to a market to buy or sell goods or services.

a. Customer relationship management
b. Disruptive technology
c. Marketing
d. Market development

18. The _____ is a United States government agency that provides support to small businesses.

The mission of the _____ is 'to maintain and strengthen the nation's economy by enabling the establishment and viability of small businesses and by assisting in the economic recovery of communities after disasters.'

The _____ makes loans directly to businesses and acts as a guarantor on bank loans. In some circumstances it also makes loans to victims of natural disasters, works to get government procurement contracts for small businesses, and assists businesses with management, technical and training issues.

a. 1990 Clean Air Act
b. 33 Strategies of War
c. 28-hour day
d. Small Business Administration

19. _____ is one of the managerial functions like planning, organizing, staffing and directing. It is an important function because it helps to check the errors and to take the corrective action so that deviation from standards are minimized and stated goals of the organization are achieved in desired manner. According to modern concepts, _____ is a foreseeing action whereas earlier concept of _____ was used only when errors were detected. _____ in management means setting standards, measuring actual performance and taking corrective action.

a. Turnover
b. Schedule of reinforcement
c. Decision tree pruning
d. Control

20. _____ was a writer, management consultant, and self-described 'social ecologist.' Widely considered to be 'the father of modern management,' his 39 books and countless scholarly and popular articles explored how humans are organized across all sectors of society--in business, government and the nonprofit world. His writings have predicted many of the major developments of the late twentieth century, including privatization and decentralization; the rise of Japan to economic world power; the decisive importance of marketing; and the emergence of the information society with its necessity of lifelong learning. In 1959, Drucker coined the term 'knowledge worker' and later in his life considered knowledge work productivity to be the next frontier of management.

a. Debora L. Spar
b. Jacques Al-Salawat Nasruddin Nasser
c. Peter Ferdinand Drucker
d. Chrissie Hynde

Chapter 1. The Foundations of Entrepreneurship

21. _____ refers to the movement of cash into or out of a business or financial product. It is usually measured during a specified, finite period of time. Measurement of _____ can be used

- to determine a project's rate of return or value. The time of _____s into and out of projects are used as inputs in financial models such as internal rate of return, and net present value.
- to determine problems with a business's liquidity. Being profitable does not necessarily mean being liquid. A company can fail because of a shortage of cash, even while profitable.
- as an alternate measure of a business's profits when it is believed that accrual accounting concepts do not represent economic realities. For example, a company may be notionally profitable but generating little operational cash (as may be the case for a company that barters its products rather than selling for cash.) In such a case, the company may be deriving additional operating cash by issuing shares evaluating default risk, re-investment requirements, etc.

_____ is a generic term used differently depending on the context. It may be defined by users for their own purposes.

a. Sweat equity
b. Gross profit margin
c. Gross profit
d. Cash flow

22. _____ is one of the four Ps of the marketing mix. The other three aspects are product, promotion, and place. It is also a key variable in microeconomic price allocation theory.

a. Transfer pricing
b. Price floor
c. Pricing
d. Penetration pricing

23. A _____ is a formal statement of a set of business goals, the reasons why they are believed attainable, and the plan for reaching those goals. It may also contain background information about the organization or team attempting to reach those goals.

The business goals may be defined for for-profit or for non-profit organizations.

a. Distributed management
b. Crisis management
c. Time management
d. Business plan

24. _____ are formal records of the financial activities of a business, person, or other entity. In British English, including United Kingdom company law, _____ are often referred to as accounts, although the term _____ is also used, particularly by accountants.

_____ provide an overview of a business or person's financial condition in both short and long term.

a. 1990 Clean Air Act
b. 33 Strategies of War
c. Financial statements
d. 28-hour day

25. In a human resources context, _____ or labor _____ is the rate at which an employer gains and loses employees. Simple ways to describe it are 'how long employees tend to stay' or 'the rate of traffic through the revolving door.' _____ is measured for individual companies and for their industry as a whole. If an employer is said to have a high _____ relative to its competitors, it means that employees of that company have a shorter average tenure than those of other companies in the same industry.

a. Turnover
b. Continuous
c. Career portfolios
d. Ten year occupational employment projection

26. In business and accounting, _____s are everything of value that is owned by a person or company. Any property or object of value that one possesses, usually considered as applicable to the payment of one's debts is considered an _____. Simplistically stated, _____s are things of value that can be readily converted into cash.

a. A4e
b. A Stake in the Outcome
c. AAAI
d. Asset

Chapter 2. Inside the Entrepreneurial Mind: From Ideas to Reality

1. _____ was a writer, management consultant, and self-described 'social ecologist.' Widely considered to be 'the father of modern management,' his 39 books and countless scholarly and popular articles explored how humans are organized across all sectors of society--in business, government and the nonprofit world. His writings have predicted many of the major developments of the late twentieth century, including privatization and decentralization; the rise of Japan to economic world power; the decisive importance of marketing; and the emergence of the information society with its necessity of lifelong learning. In 1959, Drucker coined the term 'knowledge worker' and later in his life considered knowledge work productivity to be the next frontier of management.
   a. Peter Ferdinand Drucker
   b. Jacques Al-Salawat Nasruddin Nasser
   c. Debora L. Spar
   d. Chrissie Hynde

2. _____ according to Onuoha (2007) is the practice of starting new organizations or revitalizing mature organizations, particularly new businesses generally in response to identified opportunities. _____ is often a difficult undertaking, as a vast majority of new businesses fail. Entrepreneurial activities are substantially different depending on the type of organization that is being started.
   a. Entrepreneurship
   b. A Stake in the Outcome
   c. AAAI
   d. A4e

3. _____ is a group creativity technique designed to generate a large number of ideas for the solution of a problem. The method was first popularized in the late 1930s by Alex Faickney Osborn in a book called Applied Imagination. Osborn proposed that groups could double their creative output with _____.
   a. Adam Smith
   b. Affiliation
   c. Abraham Harold Maslow
   d. Brainstorming

4. The 'business case for _____', theorizes that in a global marketplace, a company that employs a diverse workforce (both men and women, people of many generations, people from ethnically and racially diverse backgrounds etc.) is better able to understand the demographics of the marketplace it serves and is thus better equipped to thrive in that marketplace than a company that has a more limited range of employee demographics.

   An additional corollary suggests that a company that supports the _____ of its workforce can also improve employee satisfaction, productivity and retention.

   a. Diversity
   b. Trademark
   c. Kanban
   d. Virtual team

5. An _____ is an organization founded and funded by businesses that operate in a specific industry. An industry trade association participates in public relations activities such as advertising, education, political donations, lobbying and publishing, but its main focus is collaboration between companies, or standardization. Associations may offer other services, such as producing conferences, networking or charitable events or offering classes or educational materials.
   a. A4e
   b. A Stake in the Outcome
   c. AAAI
   d. Industry trade group

6. A _____ or transnational corporation is a corporation or enterprise that manages production or delivers services in more than one country. It can also be referred to as an international corporation.

   The first modern _____ is generally thought to be the Dutch East India Company, established in 1602.

a. Multinational corporation
b. Command center
c. Financial Accounting Standards Board
d. Small and medium enterprises

7. _____ is the automatic construction of physical objects using solid freeform fabrication. The first techniques for _____ became available in the late 1980s and were used to produce models and prototype parts. Today, they are used for a much wider range of applications and are even used to manufacture production quality parts in relatively small numbers.
   a. 33 Strategies of War
   b. 1990 Clean Air Act
   c. Rapid prototyping
   d. 28-hour day

8. In the United States, a _____ is a patent granted on the ornamental design of a functional item. _____s are a type of industrial design right. Ornamental designs of jewelry, furniture, beverage containers (see Fig.
   a. Reverification
   b. Design patent
   c. Robinson-Patman Act
   d. Smith Report

9. A _____ is a set of exclusive rights granted by a state to an inventor or his assignee for a limited period of time in exchange for a disclosure of an invention.

The procedure for granting _____s, the requirements placed on the _____ee and the extent of the exclusive rights vary widely between countries according to national laws and international agreements. Typically, however, a _____ application must include one or more claims defining the invention which must be new, inventive, and useful or industrially applicable.

   a. Federal Trade Commission Act
   b. Food, Drug, and Cosmetic Act
   c. Patent
   d. Labor Management Reporting and Disclosure Act

10. A _____ is a distinctive sign or indicator used by an individual, business organization, or other legal entity to identify that the products and/or services to consumers with which the _____ appears originate from a unique source and to distinguish its products or services from those of other entities.
    a. Kanban
    b. Succession planning
    c. Virtual team
    d. Trademark

11. _____ are legal property rights over creations of the mind, both artistic and commercial, and the corresponding fields of law. Under _____ law, owners are granted certain exclusive rights to a variety of intangible assets, such as musical, literary, and artistic works; ideas, discoveries and inventions; and words, phrases, symbols, and designs. Common types of _____ include copyrights, trademarks, patents, industrial design rights and trade secrets.
    a. Intellectual Property
    b. Equal Pay Act
    c. Intent
    d. Unemployment Action Center

12. _____ plant, and equipment, is a term used in accountancy for assets and property which cannot easily be converted into cash. This can be compared with current assets such as cash or bank accounts, which are described as liquid assets. In most cases, only tangible assets are referred to as fixed.
    a. 28-hour day
    b. 1990 Clean Air Act
    c. 33 Strategies of War
    d. Fixed asset

Chapter 2. Inside the Entrepreneurial Mind: From Ideas to Reality

13. _____ is an advertisement in which a particular product specifically mentions a competitor by name for the express purpose of showing why the competitor is inferior to the product naming it.

This should not be confused with parody advertisements, where a fictional product is being advertised for the purpose of poking fun at the particular advertisement, nor should it be confused with the use of a coined brand name for the purpose of comparing the product without actually naming an actual competitor. ('Wikipedia tastes better and is less filling than the Encyclopedia Galactica.')

In the 1980s, during what has been referred to as the cola wars, soft-drink manufacturer Pepsi ran a series of advertisements where people, caught on hidden camera, in a blind taste test, chose Pepsi over rival Coca-Cola.

   a. Comparative advertising
   c. 33 Strategies of War
   b. 1990 Clean Air Act
   d. 28-hour day

14. _____ exists when one firm provides goods or services to a customer with an agreement to bill them later, or receive a shipment or service from a supplier under an agreement to pay them later. It can be viewed as an essential element of capitalization in an operating business because it can reduce the required capital investment to operate the business if it is managed properly. _____ is the largest use of capital for a majority of business to business (B2B) sellers in the United States and is a critical source of capital for a majority of all businesses.
   a. Countertrade
   c. Buy-sell agreement
   b. 1990 Clean Air Act
   d. Trade credit

Chapter 3. Strategic Management and the Entrepreneur

1. _____ refers to the stock of skills and knowledge embodied in the ability to perform labor so as to produce economic value. It is the skills and knowledge gained by a worker through education and experience. Many early economic theories refer to it simply as labor, one of three factors of production, and consider it to be a fungible resource -- homogeneous and easily interchangeable.
    a. Deflation
    b. Human capital
    c. Productivity management
    d. Market structure

2. The term _____ collectively refers to all resources that determine the value and the competitiveness of an enterprise. As such, it includes as subsets the attributes that concur to building all financial statements as well as the balance sheet.
    a. A4e
    b. A Stake in the Outcome
    c. AAAI
    d. Intellectual capital

3. _____ is something that a firm can do well and that meets the following three conditions:

Competencies are things that companys execute well across several business units or product sectors.

Firms usually have few competencies, but these are usually less liable to change rapidly.

   1. It provides consumer benefits
   2. It is not easy for competitors to imitate
   3. It can be leveraged widely to many products and markets.

A _____ can take various forms, including technical/subject matter know-how, a reliable process and/or close relationships with customers and suppliers (Mascarenhas et al. 1998.)

    a. Core competency
    b. NAIRU
    c. Dominant Design
    d. Learning-by-doing

4. _____ is, in very basic words, a position a firm occupies against its competitors.

According to Michael Porter, the three methods for creating a sustainable _____ are through:

1. Cost leadership

2. Differentiation

3. Focus (economics)

    a. 28-hour day
    b. Competitive advantage
    c. Theory Z
    d. 1990 Clean Air Act

5. A _____ is a brief written statement of the purpose of a company or organization. Ideally, a _____ guides the actions of the organization, spells out its overall goal, provides a sense of direction, and guides decision making for all levels of management.

Chapter 3. Strategic Management and the Entrepreneur

_____s often contain the following:

- Purpose and aim of the organization
- The organization's primary stakeholders: clients, stockholders, etc.
- Responsibilities of the organization toward these stakeholders
- Products and services offered

In developing a _____:

- Encourage as much input as feasible from employees, volunteers, and other stakeholders
- Publicize it broadly

The _____ can be used to resolve differences between business stakeholders. Stakeholders include: employees including managers and executives, stockholders, board of directors, customers, suppliers, distributors, creditors, governments (local, state, federal, etc.), unions, competitors, NGO's, and the general public.

a. 1990 Clean Air Act
c. 33 Strategies of War
b. 28-hour day
d. Mission statement

6. _____ in marketing and strategic management is an assessment of the strengths and weaknesses of current and potential competitors. This analysis provides both an offensive and defensive strategic context through which to identify opportunities and threats. Competitor profiling coalesces all of the relevant sources of _____ into one framework in the support of efficient and effective strategy formulation, implementation, monitoring and adjustment.

a. 1990 Clean Air Act
c. Competitor or Competitive Intelligence
b. 28-hour day
d. Competitor analysis

7. A _____ is a relatively new executive level position at a corporation, company, organization typically reporting directly to the CEO or board of directors. The _____ is responsible for a brand's image, experience, and promise, and propagating it throughout all aspects of the company. The brand officer oversees marketing, advertising, design, public relations and customer service departments.

a. Director of communications
c. Chief brand officer
b. Chief executive officer
d. Purchasing manager

8. _____ is the process of comparing the cost, cycle time, productivity, or quality of a specific process or method to another that is widely considered to be an industry standard or best practice. Essentially, _____ provides a snapshot of the performance of your business and helps you understand where you are in relation to a particular standard. The result is often a business case for making changes in order to make improvements.

a. Competitive heterogeneity
c. Benchmarking
b. Cost leadership
d. Complementors

9. A _____ is a set of exclusive rights granted by a state to an inventor or his assignee for a limited period of time in exchange for a disclosure of an invention.

The procedure for granting _____s, the requirements placed on the _____ee and the extent of the exclusive rights vary widely between countries according to national laws and international agreements. Typically, however, a _____ application must include one or more claims defining the invention which must be new, inventive, and useful or industrially applicable.

a. Labor Management Reporting and Disclosure Act
b. Federal Trade Commission Act
c. Food, Drug, and Cosmetic Act
d. Patent

10. _____ is an advertisement in which a particular product specifically mentions a competitor by name for the express purpose of showing why the competitor is inferior to the product naming it.

This should not be confused with parody advertisements, where a fictional product is being advertised for the purpose of poking fun at the particular advertisement, nor should it be confused with the use of a coined brand name for the purpose of comparing the product without actually naming an actual competitor. ('Wikipedia tastes better and is less filling than the Encyclopedia Galactica.')

In the 1980s, during what has been referred to as the cola wars, soft-drink manufacturer Pepsi ran a series of advertisements where people, caught on hidden camera, in a blind taste test, chose Pepsi over rival Coca-Cola.

a. Comparative advertising
b. 28-hour day
c. 33 Strategies of War
d. 1990 Clean Air Act

11. A broad definition of _____ is the action of gathering, analyzing, and distributing information about products, customers, competitors and any aspect of the environment needed to support executives and managers in making strategic decisions for an organization.

Key points of this definitions:

1. _____ is an ethical and legal business practice. (This is important as _____ professionals emphasize that the discipline is not the same as industrial espionage which is both unethical and usually illegal.)
2. The focus is on the external business environment.
3. There is a process involved in gathering information, converting it into intelligence and then utilizing this in business decision making. _____ professionals emphasize that if the intelligence gathered is not usable (or actionable) then it is not intelligence.

A more focused definition of _____ regards it as the organizational function responsible for the early identification of risks and opportunities in the market before they become obvious. Experts also call this process the early signal analysis. This definition focuses attention on the difference between dissemination of widely available factual information (such as market statistics, financial reports, newspaper clippings) performed by functions such as libraries and information centers, and _____ which is a perspective on developments and events aimed at yielding a competitive edge.

a. 1990 Clean Air Act
b. 28-hour day
c. Competitive intelligence
d. Competitor or Competitive Intelligence

12. _____ comprises a range of practices used in an organisation to identify, create, represent, distribute and enable adoption of insights and experiences. Such insights and experiences comprise knowledge, either embodied in individuals or embedded in organisational processes or practice.

An established discipline since 1991, _____ includes courses taught in the fields of business administration, information systems, management, and library and information sciences.

a. 1990 Clean Air Act
b. 28-hour day
c. Knowledge management
d. 33 Strategies of War

13. In finance, an _____ is a contract between a buyer and a seller that gives the buyer the right--but not the obligation-- to buy or to sell a particular asset (the underlying asset) at a later day at an agreed price. In return for granting the _____, the seller collects a payment (the premium) from the buyer. A call _____ gives the buyer the right to buy the underlying asset; a put _____ gives the buyer of the _____ the right to sell the underlying asset.

a. AAAI
b. A4e
c. Option
d. A Stake in the Outcome

14. In economics, business, retail, and accounting, a _____ is the value of money that has been used up to produce something, and hence is not available for use anymore. In economics, a _____ is an alternative that is given up as a result of a decision. In business, the _____ may be one of acquisition, in which case the amount of money expended to acquire it is counted as _____.

a. Fixed costs
b. Cost
c. Cost allocation
d. Cost overrun

15. _____ is a concept developed by Michael Porter, used in business strategy. It describes a way to establish the competitive advantage. _____, in basic words, means the lowest cost of operation in the industry.

a. Strategic group
b. Strategic business unit
c. Switching cost
d. Cost leadership

16. _____ has been described as the 'process of social influence in which one person can enlist the aid and support of others in the accomplishment of a common task'. A definition more inclusive of followers comes from Alan Keith of Genentech who said '_____ is ultimately about creating a way for people to contribute to making something extraordinary happen.'

_____ is one of the most salient aspects of the organizational context. However, defining _____ has been challenging.

a. 28-hour day
b. Situational leadership
c. Leadership
d. 1990 Clean Air Act

17. The _____ is a performance management tool for measuring whether the smaller-scale operational activities of a company are aligned with its larger-scale objectives in terms of vision and strategy.

By focusing not only on financial outcomes but also on the operational, marketing and developmental inputs to these, the _____ helps provide a more comprehensive view of a business, which in turn helps organizations act in their best long-term interests. This tool is also being used to address business response to climate change and greenhouse gas emissions.

a. Management development
b. Balanced scorecard
c. Middle management
d. Commercial management

18. _____ is one of the managerial functions like planning, organizing, staffing and directing. It is an important function because it helps to check the errors and to take the corrective action so that deviation from standards are minimized and stated goals of the organization are achieved in desired manner. According to modern concepts, _____ is a foreseeing action whereas earlier concept of _____ was used only when errors were detected. _____ in management means setting standards, measuring actual performance and taking corrective action.

a. Schedule of reinforcement
b. Control
c. Turnover
d. Decision tree pruning

Chapter 4. Forms of Business Ownership and Franchising

1. _____ is the state or fact of exclusive rights and control over property, which may be an object, land/real estate or intellectual property. An _____ right is also referred to as title. The concept of _____ has existed for thousands of years and in all cultures.
   a. A Stake in the Outcome
   b. Emanation of the state
   c. Ownership
   d. A4e

2. An _____, for United States federal income tax purposes, is a corporation that makes a valid election to be taxed under Subchapter S of Chapter 1 of the Internal Revenue Code.

   In general, _____s do not pay any income taxes. Instead, the corporation's income or losses are divided among and passed through to its shareholders.

   a. 1990 Clean Air Act
   b. 28-hour day
   c. S corporation
   d. 33 Strategies of War

3. A _____ also known as a sole trader, or simply proprietorship is a type of business entity which there is only one owner and he has the final word taking all desicions by himself. All debts of the business are debts of the owner and must pay from his personal possessions. This means that the owner has unlimited liabilty.
   a. Sole proprietorship
   b. Foreign ownership
   c. Golden hello
   d. Business rule

4. A _____ is a type of business entity in which partners (owners) share with each other the profits or losses of the business. _____s are often favored over corporations for taxation purposes, as the _____ structure does not generally incur a tax on profits before it is distributed to the partners (i.e. there is no dividend tax levied.) However, depending on the _____ structure and the jurisdiction in which it operates, owners of a _____ may be exposed to greater personal liability than they would as shareholders of a corporation.
   a. Partnership
   b. Federal Employers Liability Act
   c. Due process
   d. Mediation

5. Articles of Partnership is a voluntary contract between two or among more than two persons to place their capital, labor, and skills, and corporation in business with the understanding that there will be a sharing of the profits and losses between/among partners. Outside of North America, it is normally referred to simply as a _____.

   There are also multiple sections which are often included as well in articles of partnership, based on the circumstance.

   a. Foreign Corrupt Practices Act
   b. Joint venture
   c. Reverification
   d. Partnership agreement

6. In the commercial and legal parlance of most countries, a _____ or simply a partnership, refers to an association of persons or an unincorporated company with the following major features:

   - Created by agreement, proof of existence and estoppel.
   - Formed by two or more persons
   - The owners are all personally liable for any legal actions and debts the company may face

   It is a partnership in which partners share equally in both responsibility and liability.

Chapter 4. Forms of Business Ownership and Franchising 17

Partnerships have certain default characteristics relating to both the relationship between the individual partners and (b) the relationship between the partnership and the outside world. The former can generally be overridden by agreement between the partners, whereas the latter generally cannot be.

The assets of the business are owned on behalf of the other partners, and they are each personally liable, jointly and severally, for business debts, taxes or tortious liability.

a. Prospero Business Suite
b. General partnership
c. National Center for Trauma-Informed Care
d. Business Roundtable

7. A limited partnership is a form of partnership similar to a general partnership, except that in addition to one or more general partners (GPs), there are one or more _____ It is a partnership in which only one partner is required to be a general partner.

The GPs are, in all major respects, in the same legal position as partners in a conventional firm, i.e. they have management control, share the right to use partnership property, share the profits of the firm in predefined proportions, and have joint and several liability for the debts of the partnership.

a. Limited partnership
b. Growth capital
c. Limited partners
d. Venture Capitalist

8. A _____ is a form of partnership similar to a general partnership, except that in addition to one or more general partners (GPs), there are one or more limited partners (_____s.) It is a partnership in which only one partner is required to be a general partner.

The GPs are, in all major respects, in the same legal position as partners in a conventional firm, i.e. they have management control, share the right to use partnership property, share the profits of the firm in predefined proportions, and have joint and several liability for the debts of the partnership.

a. Growth capital
b. Private equity
c. Limited Partnership
d. Pension fund

9. _____ is a concept whereby a person's financial liability is limited to a fixed sum, most commonly the value of a person's investment in a company or partnership with _____. In other words, if a company with _____ is sued, then the plaintiffs are suing the company, not its owners or investors. A shareholder in a limited company is not personally liable for any of the debts of the company, other than for the value of his investment in that company.

a. Toxic Substances Control Act
b. Privity
c. Limited liability
d. Partnership

10. In the United Kingdom _____s are governed by the _____s Act 2000 (in England and Wales and Scotland) and the _____s Act (Northern Ireland) 2002 in Northern Ireland. A UK _____ is a Corporate body - that is to say, it has a continuing legal existence independent of its Members, as compared to a Partnership which may (in England and Wales they do not) have a legal existence dependent upon its Membership.

A UK _____'s members have a collective ('Joint') responsibility, to the extent that they may agree in an '_____ agreement', but no individual ('several') responsibility for each other's actions.

a. Limited liability partnership
b. Compensation methods
c. Small and medium enterprises
d. Chief risk officer

11. The _____ , which includes its 1976 revision called the Revised _____, is a uniform act (similar to a model statute), proposed by the National Conference of Commissioners on Uniform State Laws ('NCCUSL') for the governance of business partnerships by U.S. States. The NCCUSL promulgated the original _____ in 1916 and the most recent revision in 2001.

The NCCUSL promulgated the original _____ in 1916, which is now called the _____ (1916) or _____ (1916); a 1976 revision named the Revised _____ which is also now called the _____ (1976), _____ (1976) or RUniform Limited Partnership Act (1976); a 1985 revision named _____ (1976) with 1985 Amendments, which is also now called _____ (1985) or RUniform Limited Partnership Act (1985); and a 2001 revision that was colloquially called Re-RUniform Limited Partnership Act during the drafting process but then was officially named the _____ (2001) or _____ (2001.)

a. Uniform Limited Partnership Act
b. AAAI
c. A4e
d. A Stake in the Outcome

12. _____ can refer to a law of local or limited application, passed under the authority of a higher law specifying what things may be regulated by the _____, or it can refer to the internal rules of a company or organisation.

Corporate and organizational _____s regulate only the organisation to which they apply and are generally concerned with the operation of the organisation, setting out the form, manner or procedure in which a company or organisation should be run. Corporate _____s are drafted by a corporation's founders or directors under the authority of its Charter or Articles of Incorporation.

a. Genuine Occupational Qualification
b. Bylaw
c. Racketeer Influenced and Corrupt Organizations Act
d. Fiduciary

13. _____ is a contractual right that gives its holder the option to enter a business transaction with the owner of something, according to specified terms, before the owner is entitled to enter into that transaction with a third party. In brief, the _____ is similar in concept to a call option.

An _____ can cover almost any sort of asset, including real estate, personal property, a patent license, a screenplay, or an interest in a business.

a. Right of first refusal
b. 33 Strategies of War
c. 1990 Clean Air Act
d. 28-hour day

Chapter 4. Forms of Business Ownership and Franchising

14. A mutual shareholder or _____ is an individual or company (including a corporation) that legally owns one or more shares of stock in a joint stock company. A company's shareholders collectively own that company. Thus, the typical goal of such companies is to enhance shareholder value.

   a. 1990 Clean Air Act
   b. Shareholder
   c. Free riding
   d. Stockholder

15. _____ is the imposition of two or more taxes on the same income (in the case of income taxes), asset (in the case of capital taxes), or financial transaction (in the case of sales taxes.) It refers to two distinct situations:

   - taxation of dividend income without relief or credit for taxes paid by the company paying the dividend on the income from which the dividend is paid. This arises in the so-called 'classical' system of corporate taxation, used in the United States.
   - taxation by two or more countries of the same income, asset or transaction, for example income paid by an entity of one country to a resident of a different country. The double liability is often mitigated by tax treaties between countries.

   It is not unusual for a business or individual who is resident in one country to make a taxable gain (earnings, profits) in another. This person may find that he is obliged by domestic laws to pay tax on that gain locally and pay again in the country in which the gain was made. Since this is inequitable, many nations make bilateral _____ agreements with each other.

   a. Federal Reserve Banks
   b. Tax evasion
   c. Double taxation
   d. Federal Unemployment Tax Act

16. _____, commonly known as e-commerce, consists of the buying and selling of products or services over electronic systems such as the Internet and other computer networks. The amount of trade conducted electronically has grown extraordinarily with widespread Internet usage. The use of commerce is conducted in this way, spurring and drawing on innovations in electronic funds transfer, supply chain management, Internet marketing, online transaction processing, electronic data interchange (EDI), inventory management systems, and automated data collection systems.

   a. Electronic Commerce
   b. A4e
   c. Online shopping
   d. A Stake in the Outcome

17. A _____ in the law of the vast majority of United States jurisdictions is a legal form of business company that provides limited liability to its owners. Often incorrectly called a 'limited liability corporation' (instead of company), it is a hybrid business entity having certain characteristics of both a corporation and a partnership or sole proprietorship (depending on how many owners there are.) The primary characteristic an _____ shares with a corporation is limited liability, and the primary characteristic it shares with a partnership is the availability of pass-through income taxation.

   a. Limited partners
   b. Growth capital
   c. Venture Capitalist
   d. Limited liability company

18. In law, _____ refers to the process by which a company (or part of a company) is brought to an end, and the assets and property of the company redistributed. _____ can also be referred to as winding-up or dissolution, although dissolution technically refers to the last stage of _____. The process of _____ also arises when customs, an authority or agency in a country responsible for collecting and safeguarding customs duties, determines the final computation or ascertainment of the duties or drawback accruing on an entry.

a. 1990 Clean Air Act
b. 33 Strategies of War
c. Liquidation
d. 28-hour day

19. A _____ is an entity formed between two or more parties to undertake economic activity together. The parties agree to create a new entity by both contributing equity, and they then share in the revenues, expenses, and control of the enterprise. The venture can be for one specific project only, or a continuing business relationship such as the Fuji Xerox _____.

a. Patent
b. Meritor Savings Bank v. Vinson
c. Joint venture
d. Civil Rights Act of 1991

20. An _____ is a person who has possession of an enterprise and assumes significant accountability for the inherent risks and the outcome. It is an ambitious leader who combines land, labor, and capital to create and market new goods or services. The term is a loanword from French and was first defined by the Irish economist Richard Cantillon.

a. A4e
b. A Stake in the Outcome
c. Entrepreneur
d. AAAI

21. _____ is one of the four elements of marketing mix. An organization or set of organizations (go-betweens) involved in the process of making a product or service available for use or consumption by a consumer or business user.

The other three parts of the marketing mix are product, pricing, and promotion.

a. Job creation programs
b. Distribution
c. Missing completely at random
d. Matching theory

22. _____ refers to the methods of practicing and using another person's business philosophy. The franchisor grants the independent operator the right to distribute its products, techniques, and trademarks for a percentage of gross monthly sales and a royalty fee. Various tangibles and intangibles such as national or international advertising, training, and other support services are commonly made available by the franchisor.

a. Franchising
b. 28-hour day
c. ServiceMaster
d. 1990 Clean Air Act

23. _____ is an advertisement in which a particular product specifically mentions a competitor by name for the express purpose of showing why the competitor is inferior to the product naming it.

This should not be confused with parody advertisements, where a fictional product is being advertised for the purpose of poking fun at the particular advertisement, nor should it be confused with the use of a coined brand name for the purpose of comparing the product without actually naming an actual competitor. ('Wikipedia tastes better and is less filling than the Encyclopedia Galactica.')

In the 1980s, during what has been referred to as the cola wars, soft-drink manufacturer Pepsi ran a series of advertisements where people, caught on hidden camera, in a blind taste test, chose Pepsi over rival Coca-Cola.

a. 28-hour day
b. 33 Strategies of War
c. Comparative advertising
d. 1990 Clean Air Act

Chapter 4. Forms of Business Ownership and Franchising

24. _____ is a form of communication that typically attempts to persuade potential customers to purchase or to consume more of a particular brand of product or service. 'While now central to the contemporary global economy and the reproduction of global production networks, it is only quite recently that _____ has been more than a marginal influence on patterns of sales and production. The formation of modern _____ was intimately bound up with the emergence of new forms of monopoly capitalism around the end of the 19th and beginning of the 20th century as one element in corporate strategies to create, organize and where possible control markets, especially for mass produced consumer goods.
    a. AAAI
    b. Advertising
    c. A Stake in the Outcome
    d. A4e

25. _____ is a way of expressing knowledge or belief that an event will occur or has occurred. In mathematics the concept has been given an exact meaning in _____ theory, that is used extensively in such areas of study as mathematics, statistics, finance, gambling, science, and philosophy to draw conclusions about the likelihood of potential events and the underlying mechanics of complex systems.

    The word _____ does not have a consistent direct definition.

    a. Standard deviation
    b. Statistics
    c. Time series analysis
    d. Probability

26. In economics, business, retail, and accounting, a _____ is the value of money that has been used up to produce something, and hence is not available for use anymore. In economics, a _____ is an alternative that is given up as a result of a decision. In business, the _____ may be one of acquisition, in which case the amount of money expended to acquire it is counted as _____.
    a. Fixed costs
    b. Cost allocation
    c. Cost overrun
    d. Cost

27. _____, when used as a special term, refers to various incentive plans introduced by businesses that provide direct or indirect payments to employees that depend on company's profitability in addition to employees' regular salary and bonuses. In publicly traded companies these plans typically amount to allocation of shares to employees.

    The _____ plans are based on predetermined economic sharing rules that define the split of gains between the company as a principal and the employee as an agent.

    a. Living wage
    b. Wage
    c. Federal Wage System
    d. Profit sharing

28. There are many important decisions about product and service development and marketing. In the process of product development and marketing we should focus on strategic decisions about product attributes, product branding, product packaging, product labeling and product support services. But product strategy also calls for building a _____.
    a. Context analysis
    b. Marketing strategy
    c. Product line
    d. Product bundling

29. The _____ is an independent agency of the United States government, established in 1914 by the _____ Act. Its principal mission is the promotion of 'consumer protection' and the elimination and prevention of what regulators perceive to be harmfully 'anti-competitive' business practices, such as coercive monopoly.

Chapter 4. Forms of Business Ownership and Franchising

The _____ Act was one of President Wilson's major acts against trusts.

   a. 1990 Clean Air Act
   b. 33 Strategies of War
   c. 28-hour day
   d. Federal Trade Commission

30. _____ is an abbreviation for '_____', a legal document used in the franchising process in the United States.

Franchisors must give a _____ to franchisees at least 10 business days before any contract is signed and before any money changes hands. It contains extensive information about a franchisor, which is intended to give potential franchisees enough information to make educated decisions about their investments.

   a. Uniform Franchise Offering Circular
   b. A4e
   c. AAAI
   d. A Stake in the Outcome

31. In finance, an _____ is a contract between a buyer and a seller that gives the buyer the right--but not the obligation--to buy or to sell a particular asset (the underlying asset) at a later day at an agreed price. In return for granting the _____, the seller collects a payment (the premium) from the buyer. A call _____ gives the buyer the right to buy the underlying asset; a put _____ gives the buyer of the _____ the right to sell the underlying asset.

   a. AAAI
   b. A Stake in the Outcome
   c. A4e
   d. Option

32. In a human resources context, _____ or labor _____ is the rate at which an employer gains and loses employees. Simple ways to describe it are 'how long employees tend to stay' or 'the rate of traffic through the revolving door.' _____ is measured for individual companies and for their industry as a whole. If an employer is said to have a high _____ relative to its competitors, it means that employees of that company have a shorter average tenure than those of other companies in the same industry.

   a. Career portfolios
   b. Ten year occupational employment projection
   c. Continuous
   d. Turnover

33. _____ consists of the mental process of thinking involved with the process of judging the merits of multiple options and selecting one of them for action. Some simple examples include deciding whether to get up in the morning or go back to sleep, or selecting a given route for a journey. More complex examples (often decisions that affect what a person thinks or their core beliefs) include choosing a lifestyle, religious affiliation, or political position.

   a. Groups decision making
   b. Championship mobilization
   c. Trade study
   d. Choice

34. The term '_____' refers to the concept of collecting information and attempting to spot a pattern in the information. In some fields of study, the term '_____' has more formally-defined meanings.

In project management _____ is a mathematical technique that uses historical results to predict future outcome.

   a. Regression analysis
   b. Least squares
   c. Stepwise regression
   d. Trend analysis

35. _____ is an integrated communications-based process through which individuals and communities discover that existing and newly-identified needs and wants may be satisfied by the products and services of others.

_____ is defined by the American _____ Association as the activity, set of institutions, and processes for creating, communicating, delivering, and exchanging offerings that have value for customers, clients, partners, and society at large. The term developed from the original meaning which referred literally to going to market, as in shopping, or going to a market to buy or sell goods or services.

a. Customer relationship management
b. Marketing
c. Market development
d. Disruptive technology

Chapter 5. Buying an Existing Business

1. In finance, an _____ is a contract between a buyer and a seller that gives the buyer the right--but not the obligation-- to buy or to sell a particular asset (the underlying asset) at a later day at an agreed price. In return for granting the _____, the seller collects a payment (the premium) from the buyer. A call _____ gives the buyer the right to buy the underlying asset; a put _____ gives the buyer of the _____ the right to sell the underlying asset.
   a. A4e
   b. A Stake in the Outcome
   c. AAAI
   d. Option

2. In business and accounting, _____s are everything of value that is owned by a person or company. Any property or object of value that one possesses, usually considered as applicable to the payment of one's debts is considered an _____. Simplistically stated, _____s are things of value that can be readily converted into cash.
   a. AAAI
   b. A4e
   c. A Stake in the Outcome
   d. Asset

3. _____ are defined as identifiable non-monetary assets that cannot be seen, touched or physically measured, which are created through time and/or effort and that are identifiable as a separate asset. There are two primary forms of intangibles - legal intangibles (such as trade secrets (e.g., customer lists), copyrights, patents, trademarks, and goodwill) and competitive intangibles (such as knowledge activities (know-how, knowledge), collaboration activities, leverage activities, and structural activities.) Legal intangibles are known under the generic term intellectual property and generate legal property rights defensible in a court of law.
   a. Induction programme
   b. Intangible assets
   c. Employee value proposition
   d. Interlocking directorate

4. _____ is one of a series of accounting transactions dealing with the billing of customers who owe money to a person, company or organization for goods and services that have been provided to the customer. In most business entities this is typically done by generating an invoice and mailing or electronically delivering it to the customer, who in turn must pay it within an established timeframe called credit or payment terms.

   An example of a common payment term is Net 30, meaning payment is due in the amount of the invoice 30 days from the date of invoice.

   a. Accounts receivable
   b. A Stake in the Outcome
   c. Other revenue
   d. Accumulated Depreciation

5. _____ is the price at which an asset would trade in a competitive Walrasian auction setting. _____ is often used interchangeably with open _____, fair value or fair _____, although these terms have distinct definitions in different standards, and may differ in some circumstances.

   International Valuation Standards defines _____ as 'the estimated amount for which a property should exchange on the date of valuation between a willing buyer and a willing seller in an arm's-length transaction after proper marketing wherein the parties had each acted knowledgeably, prudently, and without compulsion.'

   _____ is a concept distinct from market price, which is 'the price at which one can transact', while _____ is 'the true underlying value' according to theoretical standards.

   a. Restructuring
   b. Payback period
   c. Market value added
   d. Market value

Chapter 5. Buying an Existing Business

6. _____ in marketing and strategic management is an assessment of the strengths and weaknesses of current and potential competitors. This analysis provides both an offensive and defensive strategic context through which to identify opportunities and threats. Competitor profiling coalesces all of the relevant sources of _____ into one framework in the support of efficient and effective strategy formulation, implementation, monitoring and adjustment.
   a. Competitor or Competitive Intelligence
   b. 28-hour day
   c. Competitor analysis
   d. 1990 Clean Air Act

7. A _____ is a relatively new executive level position at a corporation, company, organization typically reporting directly to the CEO or board of directors. The _____ is responsible for a brand's image, experience, and promise, and propagating it throughout all aspects of the company. The brand officer oversees marketing, advertising, design, public relations and customer service departments.
   a. Director of communications
   b. Purchasing manager
   c. Chief executive officer
   d. Chief brand officer

8. Title _____s serve as guarantees to the recipient of property, ensuring that the recipient receives what he or she bargained for. The English _____s of title, sometimes included in deeds to real property, are that the grantor is lawfully seized (in fee simple) of the property, (2) that the grantor has the right to convey the property to the grantee, (3) that the property is conveyed without encumbrances (this _____ is frequently modified to allow for certain encumbrances), (4) that the grantor has done no act to encumber the property, (5) that the grantee shall have quiet possession of the property, and (6) that the grantor will execute such further assurances of the land as may be requisite (Nos. 3 and 4, which overlap significantly, are sometimes treated as one item.)
   a. Hostile work environment
   b. Trade secret
   c. Covenant
   d. Business valuation

9. A _____ is a clause in a loan or promissory note that stipulates that the full balance may be called due upon sale or transfer of ownership of the property used to secure the note. The lender has the right, but not the obligation, to call the note due in such a circumstance.

Virtually all recent mortgages made in the United States contain a _____.

   a. 1990 Clean Air Act
   b. Joint and several liability
   c. 28-hour day
   d. Due-on-sale clause

10. _____ is the area of law in which manufacturers, distributors, suppliers, retailers, and others who make products available to the public are held responsible for the injuries those products cause.

In the United States, the claims most commonly associated with _____ are negligence, strict liability, breach of warranty, and various consumer protection claims. The majority of _____ laws are determined at the state level and vary widely from state to state.

   a. Leave of absence
   b. Right-to-work laws
   c. Product liability
   d. Railway Labor Act

11. In financial accounting, a _____ or statement of financial position is a summary of a person's or organization's balances. Assets, liabilities and ownership equity are listed as of a specific date, such as the end of its financial year. A _____ is often described as a snapshot of a company's financial condition.

a. Balance sheet
c. 28-hour day
b. 33 Strategies of War
d. 1990 Clean Air Act

12. _____ is a company's financial statement that indicates how the revenue is transformed into the net income The purpose of the _____ is to show managers and investors whether the company made or lost money during the period being reported.

The important thing to remember about an _____ is that it represents a period of time.

a. AAAI
c. A Stake in the Outcome
b. Income statement
d. A4e

13. An _____ is a tax levied on the financial income of people, corporations, or other legal entities. Various _____ systems exist, with varying degrees of tax incidence. Income taxation can be progressive, proportional, or regressive.

a. A4e
c. Ordinary income
b. A Stake in the Outcome
d. Income tax

14. _____ refers to the movement of cash into or out of a business or financial product. It is usually measured during a specified, finite period of time. Measurement of _____ can be used

- to determine a project's rate of return or value. The time of _____s into and out of projects are used as inputs in financial models such as internal rate of return, and net present value.
- to determine problems with a business's liquidity. Being profitable does not necessarily mean being liquid. A company can fail because of a shortage of cash, even while profitable.
- as an alternate measure of a business's profits when it is believed that accrual accounting concepts do not represent economic realities. For example, a company may be notionally profitable but generating little operational cash (as may be the case for a company that barters its products rather than selling for cash.) In such a case, the company may be deriving additional operating cash by issuing shares evaluating default risk, re-investment requirements, etc.

_____ is a generic term used differently depending on the context. It may be defined by users for their own purposes.

a. Sweat equity
c. Gross profit
b. Gross profit margin
d. Cash flow

15. The phrase mergers and _____s refers to the aspect of corporate strategy, corporate finance and management dealing with the buying, selling and combining of different companies that can aid, finance, or help a growing company in a given industry grow rapidly without having to create another business entity.

An _____, also known as a takeover or a buyout, is the buying of one company (the 'target') by another. An _____ may be friendly or hostile.

a. A Stake in the Outcome
c. Acquisition
b. AAAI
d. A4e

Chapter 5. Buying an Existing Business

16. _____ is a process and a set of procedures used to estimate the economic value of an owner's interest in a business. Valuation is used by financial market participants to determine the price they are willing to pay or receive to consummate a sale of a business. In addition to estimating the selling price of a business, the same valuation tools are often used by business appraisers to resolve disputes related to estate and gift taxation, divorce litigation, allocate business purchase price among business assets, establish a formula for estimating the value of partners' ownership interest for buy-sell agreements, and many other business and legal purposes.
   - a. No-FEAR Act
   - b. Munn v. Illinois
   - c. Robinson-Patman Act
   - d. Business valuation

17. In economics, business, retail, and accounting, a _____ is the value of money that has been used up to produce something, and hence is not available for use anymore. In economics, a _____ is an alternative that is given up as a result of a decision. In business, the _____ may be one of acquisition, in which case the amount of money expended to acquire it is counted as _____.
   - a. Cost overrun
   - b. Cost allocation
   - c. Fixed costs
   - d. Cost

18. _____ or economic opportunity loss is the value of the next best alternative forgone as the result of making a decision. _____ analysis is an important part of a company's decision-making processes but is not treated as an actual cost in any financial statement. The next best thing that a person can engage in is referred to as the _____ of doing the best thing and ignoring the next best thing to be done.
   - a. Opportunity cost
   - b. AAAI
   - c. A Stake in the Outcome
   - d. A4e

19. The _____ is a bank regulation, which sets a framework on how banks and depository institutions must handle their capital. The categorization of assets and capital is highly standardized so that it can be risk weighted. Internationally, the Basel Committee on Banking Supervision housed at the Bank for International Settlements influence each country's banking _____s.
   - a. Lock box
   - b. Reserve requirement
   - c. Capital requirement
   - d. 1990 Clean Air Act

20. _____ refers to the process of screening, and selecting qualified people for a job at an organization or firm mid- and large-size organizations and companies often retain professional recruiters or outsource some of the process to _____ agencies. External _____ is the process of attracting and selecting employees from outside the organization.

    The _____ industry has four main types of agencies: employment agencies, _____ websites and job search engines, 'headhunters' for executive and professional _____, and in-house _____.
    - a. Recruitment Process Outsourcing
    - b. Recruitment
    - c. Referral recruitment
    - d. Labour hire

21. A _____ is a corporation in the United States that, for Federal income tax purposes, is taxed under 26 U.S.C. § 11 and Subchapter C (26 U.S.C.
    - a. 28-hour day
    - b. 33 Strategies of War
    - c. 1990 Clean Air Act
    - d. C corporation

22. An _____, for United States federal income tax purposes, is a corporation that makes a valid election to be taxed under Subchapter S of Chapter 1 of the Internal Revenue Code.

In general, _____s do not pay any income taxes. Instead, the corporation's income or losses are divided among and passed through to its shareholders.

a. 33 Strategies of War
b. 28-hour day
c. 1990 Clean Air Act
d. S corporation

23. A _____ is a form of partnership similar to a general partnership, except that in addition to one or more general partners (GPs), there are one or more limited partners (_____s.) It is a partnership in which only one partner is required to be a general partner.

The GPs are, in all major respects, in the same legal position as partners in a conventional firm, i.e. they have management control, share the right to use partnership property, share the profits of the firm in predefined proportions, and have joint and several liability for the debts of the partnership.

a. Pension fund
b. Growth capital
c. Private equity
d. Limited partnership

24. A _____ is a type of business entity in which partners (owners) share with each other the profits or losses of the business. _____s are often favored over corporations for taxation purposes, as the _____ structure does not generally incur a tax on profits before it is distributed to the partners (i.e. there is no dividend tax levied.) However, depending on the _____ structure and the jurisdiction in which it operates, owners of a _____ may be exposed to greater personal liability than they would as shareholders of a corporation.

a. Due process
b. Federal Employers Liability Act
c. Mediation
d. Partnership

25. _____ is the corporate management term for the act of reorganizing the legal, ownership, operational, or other structures of a company for the purpose of making it more profitable, or better organized for its present needs. Alternate reasons for _____ include a change of ownership or ownership structure, demerger repositioning debt _____ and financial _____.

a. Market value added
b. Restructuring
c. Net worth
d. Market value

Chapter 6. Building a Powerful Marketing Plan

1. _____ is an integrated communications-based process through which individuals and communities discover that existing and newly-identified needs and wants may be satisfied by the products and services of others.

_____ is defined by the American _____ Association as the activity, set of institutions, and processes for creating, communicating, delivering, and exchanging offerings that have value for customers, clients, partners, and society at large. The term developed from the original meaning which referred literally to going to market, as in shopping, or going to a market to buy or sell goods or services.

- a. Disruptive technology
- b. Customer relationship management
- c. Market development
- d. Marketing

2. A _____ is a formal statement of a set of business goals, the reasons why they are believed attainable, and the plan for reaching those goals. It may also contain background information about the organization or team attempting to reach those goals.

The business goals may be defined for for-profit or for non-profit organizations.

- a. Crisis management
- b. Time management
- c. Distributed management
- d. Business plan

3. _____ is a term used in marketing and strategic management to describe a product, service, brand, or company that has such a distinct sustainable competitive advantage that competing firms find it almost impossible to operate profitably in that industry. The existence of a _____ will eliminate almost all market entities, whether real or virtual. Many existing firms will leave the industry, thereby increasing the industry's concentration ratio.

- a. 1990 Clean Air Act
- b. 33 Strategies of War
- c. Category killer
- d. 28-hour day

4. _____ is an unconventional system of promotions that relies on time, energy and imagination rather than a big marketing budget. Typically, _____ tactics are unexpected and unconventional; consumers are targeted in unexpected places, which can make the idea that's being marketed memorable, generate buzz, and even spread virally. The term was coined and defined by Jay Conrad Levinson in his 1984 book _____.

- a. 28-hour day
- b. 1990 Clean Air Act
- c. Relationship marketing
- d. Guerrilla marketing

5. _____ is a form of marketing developed from direct response marketing campaigns conducted in the 1970s and 1980s which emphasizes customer retention and satisfaction, rather than a dominant focus on point-of-sale transactions.

_____ differs from other forms of marketing in that it recognizes the long term value to the firm of keeping customers, as opposed to direct or 'Intrusion' marketing, which focuses upon acquisition of new clients by targeting majority demographics based upon prospective client lists.

_____ refers to a long-term and mutually beneficial arrangement wherein both the buyer and seller focus on value enhancement with the goal of providing a more satisfying exchange.

- a. Guerrilla marketing
- b. 1990 Clean Air Act
- c. 28-hour day
- d. Relationship Marketing

Chapter 6. Building a Powerful Marketing Plan

6. A _____ is a business that is privately owned and operated, with a small number of employees and relatively low volume of sales. The legal definition of 'small' often varies by country and industry, but is generally under 100 employees in the United States and under 50 employees in the European Union. In comparison, the definition of mid-sized business by the number of employees is generally under 500 in the U.S. and 250 for the European Union.
   a. Pre-determined overhead rate
   b. Golden Boot Compensation
   c. Critical Success Factor
   d. Small business

7. A _____ is a written document that details the necessary actions to achieve one or more marketing objectives. It can be for a product or service, a brand, or a product line. _____s cover between one and five years.
   a. Disruptive technology
   b. Marketing strategy
   c. Market development
   d. Marketing plan

8. _____ or _____ data refers to selected population characteristics as used in government, marketing or opinion research, or the _____ profiles used in such research. Note the distinction from the term 'demography' Commonly-used _____s include race, age, income, disabilities, mobility (in terms of travel time to work or number of vehicles available), educational attainment, home ownership, employment status, and even location.
   a. Adam Smith
   b. Abraham Harold Maslow
   c. Affiliation
   d. Demographic

9. The 'business case for _____', theorizes that in a global marketplace, a company that employs a diverse workforce (both men and women, people of many generations, people from ethnically and racially diverse backgrounds etc.) is better able to understand the demographics of the marketplace it serves and is thus better equipped to thrive in that marketplace than a company that has a more limited range of employee demographics.

An additional corollary suggests that a company that supports the _____ of its workforce can also improve employee satisfaction, productivity and retention.

   a. Trademark
   b. Virtual team
   c. Kanban
   d. Diversity

10. Marketing research is a form of business research and is generally divided into two categories: consumer _____ and business-to-business (B2B) _____, which was previously known as industrial marketing research. Consumer marketing research studies the buying habits of individual people while business-to-business marketing research investigates the markets for products sold by one business to another.

Consumer _____ is a form of applied sociology that concentrates on understanding the behaviours, whims and preferences, of consumers in a market-based economy, and aims to understand the effects and comparative success of marketing campaigns.

   a. Mystery shoppers
   b. Market research
   c. Questionnaire
   d. Questionnaire construction

11. In business and accounting, _____s are everything of value that is owned by a person or company. Any property or object of value that one possesses, usually considered as applicable to the payment of one's debts is considered an _____. Simplistically stated, _____s are things of value that can be readily converted into cash.

Chapter 6. Building a Powerful Marketing Plan　31

a. AAAI
c. A Stake in the Outcome

b. A4e
d. Asset

12. An _____ is a survey of public opinion from a particular sample. _____s are usually designed to represent the opinions of a population by conducting a series of questions and then extrapolating generalities in ratio or within confidence intervals.

The first known example of an _____ was a local straw poll conducted by The Harrisburg Pennsylvanian in 1824, showing Andrew Jackson leading John Quincy Adams by 335 votes to 169 in the contest for the United States Presidency.

a. AAAI
c. A4e

b. A Stake in the Outcome
d. Opinion poll

13. The term '_____' refers to the concept of collecting information and attempting to spot a pattern in the information. In some fields of study, the term '_____' has more formally-defined meanings.

In project management _____ is a mathematical technique that uses historical results to predict future outcome.

a. Regression analysis
c. Trend analysis

b. Stepwise regression
d. Least squares

14. _____ describes the situation when output from (or information about the result of) an event or phenomenon in the past will influence the same event/phenomenon in the present or future. When an event is part of a chain of cause-and-effect that forms a circuit or loop, then the event is said to 'feed back' into itself.

_____ is also a synonym for:

- _____ signal; the information about the initial event that is the basis for subsequent modification of the event.
- _____ loop; the causal path that leads from the initial generation of the _____ signal to the subsequent modification of the event.

_____ is a mechanism, process or signal that is looped back to control a system within itself. Such a loop is called a _____ loop.

a. Feedback loop
c. Positive feedback

b. Feedback
d. 1990 Clean Air Act

15. A _____ is a form of qualitative research in which a group of people are asked about their attitude towards a product, service, concept, advertisement, idea, or packaging. Questions are asked in an interactive group setting where participants are free to talk with other group members.

Chapter 6. Building a Powerful Marketing Plan

The first _____s were created at the Bureau of Applied Social Research by associate director, sociologist Robert K. Merton.

a. Market analysis
b. Focus group
c. 1990 Clean Air Act
d. Marketing research

16. _____ refers to the methods of practicing and using another person's business philosophy. The franchisor grants the independent operator the right to distribute its products, techniques, and trademarks for a percentage of gross monthly sales and a royalty fee. Various tangibles and intangibles such as national or international advertising, training, and other support services are commonly made available by the franchisor.

a. Franchising
b. 28-hour day
c. ServiceMaster
d. 1990 Clean Air Act

17. _____ is an advertisement in which a particular product specifically mentions a competitor by name for the express purpose of showing why the competitor is inferior to the product naming it.

This should not be confused with parody advertisements, where a fictional product is being advertised for the purpose of poking fun at the particular advertisement, nor should it be confused with the use of a coined brand name for the purpose of comparing the product without actually naming an actual competitor. ('Wikipedia tastes better and is less filling than the Encyclopedia Galactica.')

In the 1980s, during what has been referred to as the cola wars, soft-drink manufacturer Pepsi ran a series of advertisements where people, caught on hidden camera, in a blind taste test, chose Pepsi over rival Coca-Cola.

a. 33 Strategies of War
b. 1990 Clean Air Act
c. 28-hour day
d. Comparative advertising

18. An _____ is a person who has possession of an enterprise and assumes significant accountability for the inherent risks and the outcome. It is an ambitious leader who combines land, labor, and capital to create and market new goods or services. The term is a loanword from French and was first defined by the Irish economist Richard Cantillon.

a. A4e
b. Entrepreneur
c. AAAI
d. A Stake in the Outcome

19. _____ is a type of private equity capital typically provided to early-stage, high-potential, growth companies in the interest of generating a return through an eventual realization event such as an IPO or trade sale of the company. _____ investments are generally made as cash in exchange for shares in the invested company. It is typical for _____ investors to identify and back companies in high technology industries such as biotechnology and ICT.

a. Private equity
b. Limited liability corporation
c. Seed round
d. Venture capital

20. Wholesaling, jobbing to industrial, commercial, institutional or to other _____ and related subordinated services.

Chapter 6. Building a Powerful Marketing Plan 33

According to the United Nations Statistics Division, 'wholesale' is the resale (sale without transformation) of new and used goods to retailers, to industrial, commercial, institutional or professional users or involves acting as an agent or broker in buying merchandise for such persons or companies. _____ frequently physically assemble, sort and grade goods in large lots, break bulk, repack and redistribute in smaller lots.

a. Wholesalers
b. Packaging
c. Supply chain management
d. Supply chain

21. _____ according to Onuoha (2007) is the practice of starting new organizations or revitalizing mature organizations, particularly new businesses generally in response to identified opportunities. _____ is often a difficult undertaking, as a vast majority of new businesses fail. Entrepreneurial activities are substantially different depending on the type of organization that is being started.

a. A Stake in the Outcome
b. Entrepreneurship
c. AAAI
d. A4e

22. _____ consists of the processes a company uses to track and organize its contacts with its current and prospective customers. _____ software is used to support these processes; information about customers and customer interactions can be entered, stored and accessed by employees in different company departments. Typical _____ goals are to improve services provided to customers, and to use customer contact information for targeted marketing.

a. Disruptive technology
b. Marketing plan
c. Customer relationship management
d. Green marketing

23. _____ is the process of extracting hidden patterns from data. As more data is gathered, with the amount of data doubling every three years, _____ is becoming an increasingly important tool to transform this data into information. It is commonly used in a wide range of profiling practices, such as marketing, surveillance, fraud detection and scientific discovery.

a. Data mining
b. 28-hour day
c. Decision tree learning
d. 1990 Clean Air Act

24. The loyalty business model is a business model used in strategic management in which company resources are employed so as to increase the loyalty of customers and other stakeholders in the expectation that corporate objectives will be met or surpassed. A typical example of this type of model is: quality of product or service leads to customer satisfaction, which leads to _____, which leads to profitability.

Fredrick Reichheld (1996) expanded the loyalty business model beyond customers and employees.

a. 33 Strategies of War
b. 1990 Clean Air Act
c. Customer loyalty
d. 28-hour day

25. In decision theory and estimation theory, the _____ of an estimator, $\hat{\theta}$, of an unknown parameter of the distribution, θ, is the expected value of the loss function

Chapter 6. Building a Powerful Marketing Plan

$$R(\theta, \hat{\theta}) = \mathbb{E}_\theta L(\theta, \hat{\theta}) = \int L(\theta, \hat{\theta})\, dP_\theta.$$

where dP_θ is a probability measure parametrized by θ.

- For a scalar parameter θ and a quadratic loss function,

$$L(\theta, \hat{\theta}) = (\theta - \hat{\theta})^2$$

the _____ function becomes the mean squared error of the estimate,

$$R(\theta, \hat{\theta}) = E_\theta(\theta - \hat{\theta})^2$$

- In density estimation, the unknown parameter is probability density itself. The loss function is typically chosen to be a norm in an appropriate function space. For example, for L^2 norm,

$$L(f, \hat{f}) = \|f - \hat{f}\|_2^2$$

the _____ function becomes the mean integrated squared error

$$R(f, \hat{f}) = E\|f - \hat{f}\|^2$$

a. Financial modeling
c. Risk aversion
b. Linear model
d. Risk

26. A _____ is a type of business entity in which partners (owners) share with each other the profits or losses of the business. _____s are often favored over corporations for taxation purposes, as the _____ structure does not generally incur a tax on profits before it is distributed to the partners (i.e. there is no dividend tax levied.) However, depending on the _____ structure and the jurisdiction in which it operates, owners of a _____ may be exposed to greater personal liability than they would as shareholders of a corporation.
    a. Federal Employers Liability Act
    c. Partnership
    b. Due process
    d. Mediation

27. A _____ is the subset of the market on which a specific product is focusing on; Therefore the market niche defines the specific product features aimed at satisfying specific market needs, as well as the price range, production quality and the demographics that is intended to impact.

Every single product that is on sale can be defined by its _____. As of special note, the products aimed at a wide demographics audience, with the resulting low price (due to Price elasticity of demand), are said to belong to the Mainstream niche, in practice referred only as Mainstream or of high demand.

a. Private placement
b. Niche market
c. Labor intensive
d. Choquet integral

28. _____ is the largest book retailer in the United States, operating mainly through its Barnes ' Noble Booksellers chain of bookstores headquartered in lower Fifth Avenue in Manhattan.

The company operates the chain of small 'B.

a. 1990 Clean Air Act
b. Barnes ' Noble, Inc.
c. 28-hour day
d. 33 Strategies of War

29. In probability theory, a probability distribution is called _____ if its cumulative distribution function is _____. This is equivalent to saying that for random variables X with the distribution in question, Pr[X = a] = 0 for all real numbers a, i.e.: the probability that X attains the value a is zero, for any number a. If the distribution of X is _____ then X is called a _____ random variable.

a. Pay Band
b. Connectionist expert systems
c. Continuous
d. Decision tree pruning

30. _____ is a management process whereby delivery (customer valued) processes are constantly evaluated and improved in the light of their efficiency, effectiveness and flexibility.

Some see it as a meta process for most management systems (Business Process Management, Quality Management, Project Management). Deming saw it as part of the 'system' whereby feedback from the process and customer were evaluated against organisational goals.

a. Sole proprietorship
b. Continuous Improvement Process
c. Critical Success Factor
d. First-mover advantage

31. In economics, business, retail, and accounting, a _____ is the value of money that has been used up to produce something, and hence is not available for use anymore. In economics, a _____ is an alternative that is given up as a result of a decision. In business, the _____ may be one of acquisition, in which case the amount of money expended to acquire it is counted as _____.

a. Cost allocation
b. Cost overrun
c. Fixed costs
d. Cost

32. The concept of quality costs is a means to quantify the total _____-related efforts and deficiencies. It was first described by Armand V. Feigenbaum in a 1956 Harvard Business Review article.

Prior to its introduction, the general perception was that higher quality requires higher costs, either by buying better materials or machines or by hiring more labor.

a. Cost accounting
b. Fixed costs
c. Quality costs
d. Cost of quality

Chapter 6. Building a Powerful Marketing Plan

33. _____ is a business management strategy aimed at embedding awareness of quality in all organizational processes. _____ has been widely used in manufacturing, education, hospitals, call centers, government, and service industries, as well as NASA space and science programs.

As defined by the International Organization for Standardization (ISO):

'_____ is a management approach for an organization, centered on quality, based on the participation of all its members and aiming at long-term success through customer satisfaction, and benefits to all members of the organization and to society.' ISO 8402:1994

One major aim is to reduce variation from every process so that greater consistency of effort is obtained. (Royse, D., Thyer, B., Padgett D., ' Logan T., 2006)

a. Quality management
b. 28-hour day
c. 1990 Clean Air Act
d. Total quality management

34. _____ can be considered to have three main components: quality control, quality assurance and quality improvement. _____ is focused not only on product quality, but also the means to achieve it. _____ therefore uses quality assurance and control of processes as well as products to achieve more consistent quality.

a. Quality management
b. 28-hour day
c. Total quality management
d. 1990 Clean Air Act

35. A _____ is a commercial building for storage of goods. _____s are used by manufacturers, importers, exporters, wholesalers, transport businesses, customs, etc. They are usually large plain buildings in industrial areas of cities and towns.

a. 28-hour day
b. 33 Strategies of War
c. Warehouse
d. 1990 Clean Air Act

36. _____ is the provision of service to customers before, during and after a purchase.

According to Turban et al. (2002), '_____ is a series of activities designed to enhance the level of customer satisfaction - that is, the feeling that a product or service has met the customer expectation.'

Its importance varies by product, industry and customer; defective or broken merchandise can be exchanged, often only with a receipt and within a specified time frame.

a. 1990 Clean Air Act
b. Service rate
c. 28-hour day
d. Customer service

37. _____, a business term, is a measure of how products and services supplied by a company meet or surpass customer expectation. It is seen as a key performance indicator within business and is part of the four perspectives of a Balanced Scorecard.

In a competitive marketplace where businesses compete for customers, _____ is seen as a key differentiator and increasingly has become a key element of business strategy.

Chapter 6. Building a Powerful Marketing Plan

a. Foreign ownership
c. Critical Success Factor
b. Horizontal integration
d. Customer satisfaction

38. A _____ is a name or trademark connected with a product or producer. _____s have become increasingly important components of culture and the economy, now being described as 'cultural accessories and personal philosophies'.

Some people distinguish the psychological aspect of a _____ from the experiential aspect.

a. Brand awareness
c. Brand loyalty
b. Brand extension
d. Brand

39. _____ is one of the managerial functions like planning, organizing, staffing and directing. It is an important function because it helps to check the errors and to take the corrective action so that deviation from standards are minimized and stated goals of the organization are achieved in desired manner. According to modern concepts, _____ is a foreseeing action whereas earlier concept of _____ was used only when errors were detected. _____ in management means setting standards, measuring actual performance and taking corrective action.

a. Decision tree pruning
c. Schedule of reinforcement
b. Turnover
d. Control

40. _____ Management is the succession of strategies used by management as a product goes through its _____. The conditions in which a product is sold changes over time and must be managed as it moves through its succession of stages.

The _____ goes through many phases, involves many professional disciplines, and requires many skills, tools and processes.

a. Job hunting
c. Strategic Alliance
b. Golden handshake
d. Product life cycle

41. The _____ is generally accepted as the use and specification of the 'four P's' describing the strategic position of a product in the marketplace. One version of the _____ originated in 1948 when James Culliton said that a marketing decision should be a result of something similar to a recipe. This version was used in 1953 when Neil Borden, in his American Marketing Association presidential address, took the recipe idea one step further and coined the term 'marketing-mix'.

a. Marketing mix
c. 28-hour day
b. 1990 Clean Air Act
d. 33 Strategies of War

42. _____ is one of the four elements of marketing mix. An organization or set of organizations (go-betweens) involved in the process of making a product or service available for use or consumption by a consumer or business user.

The other three parts of the marketing mix are product, pricing, and promotion.

a. Missing completely at random
c. Job creation programs
b. Distribution
d. Matching theory

Chapter 6. Building a Powerful Marketing Plan

43. _____ is a broad label that refers to any individuals or households that use goods and services generated within the economy. The concept of a _____ is used in different contexts, so that the usage and significance of the term may vary.

Typically when business people and economists talk of _____s they are talking about person as _____, an aggregated commodity item with little individuality other than that expressed in the buy/not-buy decision.

 a. 28-hour day   b. 1990 Clean Air Act
 c. Consumer   d. 33 Strategies of War

44. In economics, _____ is a measure of the relative satisfaction from consumption of various goods and services. Given this measure, one may speak meaningfully of increasing or decreasing _____, and thereby explain economic behavior in terms of attempts to increase one's _____. For illustrative purposes, changes in _____ are sometimes expressed in units called utils.

 a. Ordinal utility   b. Indirect utility function
 c. A Stake in the Outcome   d. Utility

Chapter 7. E-Commerce and the Entrepreneur

1. _____, commonly known as e-commerce, consists of the buying and selling of products or services over electronic systems such as the Internet and other computer networks. The amount of trade conducted electronically has grown extraordinarily with widespread Internet usage. The use of commerce is conducted in this way, spurring and drawing on innovations in electronic funds transfer, supply chain management, Internet marketing, online transaction processing, electronic data interchange (EDI), inventory management systems, and automated data collection systems.
   a. Online shopping
   b. Electronic Commerce
   c. A4e
   d. A Stake in the Outcome

2. An _____ is a person who has possession of an enterprise and assumes significant accountability for the inherent risks and the outcome. It is an ambitious leader who combines land, labor, and capital to create and market new goods or services. The term is a loanword from French and was first defined by the Irish economist Richard Cantillon.
   a. A4e
   b. A Stake in the Outcome
   c. Entrepreneur
   d. AAAI

3. _____ is an advertisement in which a particular product specifically mentions a competitor by name for the express purpose of showing why the competitor is inferior to the product naming it.

   This should not be confused with parody advertisements, where a fictional product is being advertised for the purpose of poking fun at the particular advertisement, nor should it be confused with the use of a coined brand name for the purpose of comparing the product without actually naming an actual competitor. ('Wikipedia tastes better and is less filling than the Encyclopedia Galactica.')

   In the 1980s, during what has been referred to as the cola wars, soft-drink manufacturer Pepsi ran a series of advertisements where people, caught on hidden camera, in a blind taste test, chose Pepsi over rival Coca-Cola.

   a. 33 Strategies of War
   b. Comparative advertising
   c. 1990 Clean Air Act
   d. 28-hour day

4. _____ is a term used to describe the demographic cohort following Generation X. Its members are often referred to as 'Millennials' or 'Echo Boomers') . There are no precise dates for when Gen Y begins and ends. Most commentators use dates from the early 1980s to early 1990s.
   a. Generation Y
   b. Giovanni Agnelli
   c. Benjamin R. Barber
   d. David Wittig

5. _____, commonly referred to as 'eBusiness' or 'e-Business', may be defined as the utilization of information and communication technologies (ICT) in support of all the activities of business. Commerce constitutes the exchange of products and services between businesses, groups and individuals and hence can be seen as one of the essential activities of any business. Hence, electronic commerce or eCommerce focuses on the use of ICT to enable the external activities and relationships of the business with individuals, groups and other businesses .
   a. A4e
   b. AAAI
   c. A Stake in the Outcome
   d. Electronic Business

6. _____ is the provision of service to customers before, during and after a purchase.

   According to Turban et al. (2002), '_____ is a series of activities designed to enhance the level of customer satisfaction - that is, the feeling that a product or service has met the customer expectation.'

Its importance varies by product, industry and customer; defective or broken merchandise can be exchanged, often only with a receipt and within a specified time frame.

a. 28-hour day
b. Service rate
c. 1990 Clean Air Act
d. Customer service

7. A _____ is a part of most corporations where tasks dedicated to running the company itself take place. The term comes from the building layout of early companies where the front office would contain the sales and other customer-facing staff and the _____ would be those manufacturing or developing the products or involved in administration but without being seen by customers. Although the operations of a _____ are usually not given a lot of consideration, they are a major contributor to a business.

a. Policies and procedures
b. Sole proprietorship
c. Featherbedding
d. Back office

8. _____ describes commerce transactions between businesses, such as between a manufacturer and a wholesaler, or between a wholesaler and a retailer. Contrasting terms are business-to-consumer (B2C) and business-to-government (B2G.)

The volume of B2B transactions is much higher than the volume of B2C transactions.

a. Market environment
b. Product bundling
c. Category management
d. Business-to-business

9. _____, commonly abbreviated to Gen X, is a term used to refer to a generational cohort of children born after the baby boom ended and usually prior to the 1980s

The term _____ has been used in demography, the social sciences, and marketing, though it is most often used in popular culture.

In the U.S. _____ was originally referred to as the 'baby bust' generation because of the drop in the birth rate following the baby boom.

a. Generation X
b. Abraham Harold Maslow
c. Adam Smith
d. Affiliation

10. _____ is an integrated communications-based process through which individuals and communities discover that existing and newly-identified needs and wants may be satisfied by the products and services of others.

_____ is defined by the American _____ Association as the activity, set of institutions, and processes for creating, communicating, delivering, and exchanging offerings that have value for customers, clients, partners, and society at large. The term developed from the original meaning which referred literally to going to market, as in shopping, or going to a market to buy or sell goods or services.

Chapter 7. E-Commerce and the Entrepreneur

a. Marketing
c. Market development
b. Customer relationship management
d. Disruptive technology

11. _____ or promotional products refers to articles of merchandise that are used in marketing and communication programs. These items are usually imprinted with a company's name, logo or slogan, and given away at trade shows, conferences, and as part of guerrilla marketing campaigns.

Almost anything can be branded with a company's name or logo and used for promotion.

a. Promotional items
c. 1990 Clean Air Act
b. 33 Strategies of War
d. 28-hour day

12. A _____ is a formal relationship between two or more parties to pursue a set of agreed upon goals or to meet a critical business need while remaining independent organizations.

Partners may provide the _____ with resources such as products, distribution channels, manufacturing capability, project funding, capital equipment, knowledge, expertise, or intellectual property. The alliance is a cooperation or collaboration which aims for a synergy where each partner hopes that the benefits from the alliance will be greater than those from individual efforts.

a. Farmshoring
c. Process automation
b. Golden parachute
d. Strategic alliance

13. _____ is a form of communication that typically attempts to persuade potential customers to purchase or to consume more of a particular brand of product or service. 'While now central to the contemporary global economy and the reproduction of global production networks, it is only quite recently that _____ has been more than a marginal influence on patterns of sales and production. The formation of modern _____ was intimately bound up with the emergence of new forms of monopoly capitalism around the end of the 19th and beginning of the 20th century as one element in corporate strategies to create, organize and where possible control markets, especially for mass produced consumer goods.

a. AAAI
c. A4e
b. A Stake in the Outcome
d. Advertising

14. The loyalty business model is a business model used in strategic management in which company resources are employed so as to increase the loyalty of customers and other stakeholders in the expectation that corporate objectives will be met or surpassed. A typical example of this type of model is: quality of product or service leads to customer satisfaction, which leads to _____, which leads to profitability.

Fredrick Reichheld (1996) expanded the loyalty business model beyond customers and employees.

a. 33 Strategies of War
c. 1990 Clean Air Act
b. 28-hour day
d. Customer loyalty

15. _____ is the measurement, collection, analysis and reporting of internet data for purposes of understanding and optimizing web usage.

There are two categories of _____; off-site and on-site _____.

Off-site _____ refers to web measurement and analysis irrespective of whether you own or maintain a website. On-site _____ measure a visitor's journey once on your website.

a. 28-hour day
b. 33 Strategies of War
c. 1990 Clean Air Act
d. Web analytics

16. _____ is the process of filtering for information or patterns using techniques involving collaboration among multiple agents, viewpoints, data sources, etc. Applications of _____ typically involve very large data sets. _____ methods have been applied to many different kinds of data including sensing and monitoring data - such as in mineral exploration, environmental sensing over large areas or multiple sensors; financial data - such as financial service institutions that integrate many financial sources; or in electronic commerce and web 2.0 applications where the focus is on user data, etc.

a. 28-hour day
b. 33 Strategies of War
c. 1990 Clean Air Act
d. Collaborative filtering

17. _____ is the intelligence of machines and the branch of computer science which aims to create it. Major _____ textbooks define the field as 'the study and design of intelligent agents,' where an intelligent agent is a system that perceives its environment and takes actions which maximize its chances of success. John McCarthy, who coined the term in 1956, defines it as 'the science and engineering of making intelligent machines.'

The field was founded on the claim that a central property of human beings, intelligence--the sapience of Homo sapiens--can be so precisely described that it can be simulated by a machine.

a. A Stake in the Outcome
b. AAAI
c. Artificial intelligence
d. A4e

18. In economics, business, retail, and accounting, a _____ is the value of money that has been used up to produce something, and hence is not available for use anymore. In economics, a _____ is an alternative that is given up as a result of a decision. In business, the _____ may be one of acquisition, in which case the amount of money expended to acquire it is counted as _____.

a. Fixed costs
b. Cost
c. Cost allocation
d. Cost overrun

19. _____ refers to the movement of cash into or out of a business or financial product. It is usually measured during a specified, finite period of time. Measurement of _____ can be used

- to determine a project's rate of return or value. The time of _____s into and out of projects are used as inputs in financial models such as internal rate of return, and net present value.
- to determine problems with a business's liquidity. Being profitable does not necessarily mean being liquid. A company can fail because of a shortage of cash, even while profitable.
- as an alternate measure of a business's profits when it is believed that accrual accounting concepts do not represent economic realities. For example, a company may be notionally profitable but generating little operational cash (as may be the case for a company that barters its products rather than selling for cash.) In such a case, the company may be deriving additional operating cash by issuing shares evaluating default risk, re-investment requirements, etc.

Chapter 7. E-Commerce and the Entrepreneur

_____ is a generic term used differently depending on the context. It may be defined by users for their own purposes.

a. Cash flow
c. Gross profit

b. Sweat equity
d. Gross profit margin

20. A _____ is typically described as a deliberate plan of action to guide decisions and achieve rational outcome(s.) However, the term may also be used to denote what is actually done, even though it is unplanned.

The term may apply to government, private sector organizations and groups, and individuals.

a. 1990 Clean Air Act
c. 33 Strategies of War

b. 28-hour day
d. Policy

21. A _____ is the return of funds to a consumer, forcibly initiated by the consumer's issuing bank. Specifically, it is the reversal of a prior outbound transfer of funds from a consumer's bank account or line of credit.

The _____ mechanism exists primarily for consumer protection.

a. 28-hour day
c. 33 Strategies of War

b. 1990 Clean Air Act
d. Chargeback

Chapter 8. Integrated Marketing Communications and Pricing Strategies

1. _____ is an integrated communications-based process through which individuals and communities discover that existing and newly-identified needs and wants may be satisfied by the products and services of others.

_____ is defined by the American _____ Association as the activity, set of institutions, and processes for creating, communicating, delivering, and exchanging offerings that have value for customers, clients, partners, and society at large. The term developed from the original meaning which referred literally to going to market, as in shopping, or going to a market to buy or sell goods or services.

   a. Disruptive technology
   c. Customer relationship management
   b. Market development
   d. Marketing

2. _____s (or MarCom or Integrated _____s) are messages and related media used to communicate with a market. Those who practice advertising, branding, direct marketing, graphic design, marketing, packaging, promotion, publicity, sponsorship, public relations, sales, sales promotion and online marketing are termed marketing communicators, _____ managers, or more briefly as marcom managers.

Traditionally, _____ practitioners focus on the creation and execution of printed marketing collateral; however, academic and professional research developed the practice to use strategic elements of branding and marketing in order to ensure consistency of message delivery throughout an organization.

   a. Thomas Dale DeLay
   c. Adam Smith
   b. Abraham Harold Maslow
   d. Marketing communication

3. The _____ is a marketing concept that was first proposed as a theory to explain a pattern among successful advertising campaigns of the early 1940s. It states that such campaigns made unique propositions to the customer and that this convinced them to switch brands. The term was invented by Rosser Reeves of Ted Bates ' Company.
   a. AAAI
   c. Unique selling proposition
   b. A Stake in the Outcome
   d. A4e

4. _____ is a form of communication that typically attempts to persuade potential customers to purchase or to consume more of a particular brand of product or service. 'While now central to the contemporary global economy and the reproduction of global production networks, it is only quite recently that _____ has been more than a marginal influence on patterns of sales and production. The formation of modern _____ was intimately bound up with the emergence of new forms of monopoly capitalism around the end of the 19th century and beginning of the 20th century as one element in corporate strategies to create, organize and where possible control markets, especially for mass produced consumer goods.
   a. AAAI
   c. Advertising
   b. A Stake in the Outcome
   d. A4e

5. _____ , also referred to simply as a 'public offering' or 'flotation,' is when a company issues common stock or shares to the public for the first time. They are often issued by smaller, younger companies seeking capital to expand, but can also be done by large privately-owned companies looking to become publicly traded.

In an _____ the issuer may obtain the assistance of an underwriting firm, which helps it determine what type of security to issue (common or preferred), best offering price and time to bring it to market.

Chapter 8. Integrated Marketing Communications and Pricing Strategies

a. Initial public offering
b. Occupational Safety and Health Administration
c. Unemployment insurance
d. Outsourcing

6. In decision analysis, the _____ is a test of how well a model element is defined. Although nothing (outside a formal system) can be completely defined, the _____ allows the decision participants to determine whether such elements as variables, events, outcomes, and alternatives are sufficiently well defined to make the decision at hand. In general, a model element is well defined is a knowledgeable individual can answer questions about the model element without asking further clarifying questions.
a. 33 Strategies of War
b. Clarity test
c. 28-hour day
d. 1990 Clean Air Act

7. _____ refers to the movement of cash into or out of a business or financial product. It is usually measured during a specified, finite period of time. Measurement of _____ can be used

- to determine a project's rate of return or value. The time of _____s into and out of projects are used as inputs in financial models such as internal rate of return, and net present value.
- to determine problems with a business's liquidity. Being profitable does not necessarily mean being liquid. A company can fail because of a shortage of cash, even while profitable.
- as an alternate measure of a business's profits when it is believed that accrual accounting concepts do not represent economic realities. For example, a company may be notionally profitable but generating little operational cash (as may be the case for a company that barters its products rather than selling for cash.) In such a case, the company may be deriving additional operating cash by issuing shares evaluating default risk, re-investment requirements, etc.

_____ is a generic term used differently depending on the context. It may be defined by users for their own purposes.

a. Gross profit margin
b. Sweat equity
c. Gross profit
d. Cash flow

8. _____ is the practice of managing the flow of information between an organization and its publics. _____ gains an organization or individual exposure to their audiences using topics of public interest and news items that do not require direct payment. Because _____ places exposure in credible third-party outlets, it offers a third-party legitimacy that advertising does not have.
a. Two-way communication
b. 1990 Clean Air Act
c. 28-hour day
d. Public relations

9. A _____ is a business that is privately owned and operated, with a small number of employees and relatively low volume of sales. The legal definition of 'small' often varies by country and industry, but is generally under 100 employees in the United States and under 50 employees in the European Union. In comparison, the definition of mid-sized business by the number of employees is generally under 500 in the U.S. and 250 for the European Union.
a. Golden Boot Compensation
b. Pre-determined overhead rate
c. Critical Success Factor
d. Small business

10. _____ is one of the four Ps of the marketing mix. The other three aspects are product, promotion, and place. It is also a key variable in microeconomic price allocation theory.

Chapter 8. Integrated Marketing Communications and Pricing Strategies

a. Price floor
b. Pricing
c. Penetration pricing
d. Transfer pricing

11. In economics, business, retail, and accounting, a _____ is the value of money that has been used up to produce something, and hence is not available for use anymore. In economics, a _____ is an alternative that is given up as a result of a decision. In business, the _____ may be one of acquisition, in which case the amount of money expended to acquire it is counted as _____.

a. Cost overrun
b. Fixed costs
c. Cost allocation
d. Cost

12. In finance, an _____ is a contract between a buyer and a seller that gives the buyer the right--but not the obligation--to buy or to sell a particular asset (the underlying asset) at a later day at an agreed price. In return for granting the _____, the seller collects a payment (the premium) from the buyer. A call _____ gives the buyer the right to buy the underlying asset; a put _____ gives the buyer of the _____ the right to sell the underlying asset.

a. A4e
b. AAAI
c. A Stake in the Outcome
d. Option

13. _____ are long-format television commercials, typically five minutes or longer.. _____ are also known as paid programming (or teleshopping in Europe.) Originally, they were a phenomenon that started in the United States where they were typically shown overnight (usually 2:00 a.m. to 6:00 a.m.)

a. A4e
b. AAAI
c. A Stake in the Outcome
d. Infomercials

14. _____ systems are rule-based systems that are able to automatically provide solutions to repetitive management problems (Turban, Leidner, McLean and Wetherbe, 2007.) _____s are very closely related to business informatics and business analytics.

_____ systems are based on business rules.

a. Entertainment Management
b. Efficient Consumer Response
c. Executive development
d. Automated decision support

15. _____ is a sub-discipline and type of marketing. There are two main definitional characteristics which distinguish it from other types of marketing. The first is that it attempts to send its messages directly to consumers, without the use of intervening media.

a. 28-hour day
b. Direct Marketing
c. Guthy-Renker
d. 1990 Clean Air Act

16. _____ generally refers to a list of all planned expenses and revenues. It is a plan for saving and spending. A _____ is an important concept in microeconomics, which uses a _____ line to illustrate the trade-offs between two or more goods.

a. 28-hour day
b. 1990 Clean Air Act
c. Budget
d. 33 Strategies of War

Chapter 8. Integrated Marketing Communications and Pricing Strategies   47

17. _____ or cause-related marketing refers to a type of marketing involving the cooperative efforts of a 'for profit' business and a non-profit organization for mutual benefit. The term is sometimes used more broadly and generally to refer to any type of marketing effort for social and other charitable causes, including in-house marketing efforts by non-profit organizations. _____ differs from corporate giving (philanthropy) as the latter generally involves a specific donation that is tax deductible, while _____ is a marketing relationship generally not based on a donation.
- a. Relationship marketing
- b. 1990 Clean Air Act
- c. 28-hour day
- d. Cause marketing

18. _____ is a financial mechanism in which a debtor obtains the right to delay payments to a creditor, for a defined period of time, in exchange for a charge or fee. Essentially, the party that owes money in the present purchases the right to delay the payment until some future date. The discount, or charge, is simply the difference between the original amount owed in the present and the amount that has to be paid in the future to settle the debt.
- a. Discounting
- b. Financial modeling
- c. Linear model
- d. Ruin theory

19. In accounting, _____ or sales profit is the difference between revenue and the cost of making a product or providing a service, before deducting overhead, payroll, taxation, and interest payments. Note that this is different from operating profit (earnings before interest and taxes.)

Net sales are calculated:

Net sales = Sales - Sales returns and allowances.

- a. Gross profit
- b. Cash flow
- c. Gross profit margin
- d. Capital budgeting

20. _____ is a financial ratio used to assess the profitability of a firm's core activities, excluding fixed costs.

The general calculation is:

[×]

The _____ is related to the net profit margin, which assesses the profitability of an organization after including fixed costs.

_____ indicates the relationship between net sales revenue and the cost of goods sold.

- a. Capital structure
- b. Shareholder value
- c. Gross profit margin
- d. Sweat equity

21. _____ is a term used in business to indicate a state of intense competitive rivalry accompanied by a multi-lateral series of price reduction. One competitor will lower its price, then others will lower their prices to match. If one of them reduces their price again, a new round of reductions starts.

48 *Chapter 8. Integrated Marketing Communications and Pricing Strategies*

    a. Price floor
    b. Price war
    c. Price ceiling
    d. Pricing

22. _____, net margin, net _____ or net profit ratio all refer to a measure of profitability. It is calculated by finding the net profit as a percentage of the revenue.

$$\text{Net profit margin} = \frac{\text{Net profit (after taxes)}}{\text{Revenue}} \times 100\%$$

The _____ is mostly used for internal comparison.

    a. Net profit margin
    b. Profit maximization
    c. 1990 Clean Air Act
    d. Profit margin

23. _____ is one of the four growth strategies of the Product-Market Growth Matrix defined by Ansoff. _____ occurs when a company enters/penetrates a market with current products. The best way to achieve this is by gaining competitors' customers (part of their market share.)

    a. 33 Strategies of War
    b. 28-hour day
    c. 1990 Clean Air Act
    d. Market penetration

24. _____ is the pricing technique of setting a relatively low initial entry price, often lower than the eventual market price, to attract new customers. The strategy works on the expectation that customers will switch to the new brand because of the lower price. _____ is most commonly associated with a marketing objective of increasing market share or sales volume, rather than to make profit in the short term.

    a. Price war
    b. Transfer pricing
    c. Pricing objectives
    d. Penetration pricing

25. In economics, _____ is the desire to own something and the ability to pay for it. The term _____ signifies the ability or the willingness to buy a particular commodity at a given point of time.

    a. 33 Strategies of War
    b. 28-hour day
    c. 1990 Clean Air Act
    d. Demand

26. _____ is an advertisement in which a particular product specifically mentions a competitor by name for the express purpose of showing why the competitor is inferior to the product naming it.

This should not be confused with parody advertisements, where a fictional product is being advertised for the purpose of poking fun at the particular advertisement, nor should it be confused with the use of a coined brand name for the purpose of comparing the product without actually naming an actual competitor. ('Wikipedia tastes better and is less filling than the Encyclopedia Galactica.')

In the 1980s, during what has been referred to as the cola wars, soft-drink manufacturer Pepsi ran a series of advertisements where people, caught on hidden camera, in a blind taste test, chose Pepsi over rival Coca-Cola.

Chapter 8. Integrated Marketing Communications and Pricing Strategies

a. 1990 Clean Air Act
b. 33 Strategies of War
c. Comparative advertising
d. 28-hour day

27. _____ is a lightweight markup language, originally created by John Gruber and Aaron Swartz to help maximum readability and 'publishability' of both its input and output forms. The language takes many cues from existing conventions for marking up plain text in email. _____ converts its marked-up text input to valid, well-formed XHTML and replaces left-pointing angle brackets ('<') and ampersands with their corresponding character entity references.
   a. 1990 Clean Air Act
   b. Markdown
   c. 33 Strategies of War
   d. 28-hour day

28. _____ is the difference between the cost of a good or service and its selling price. A _____ is added on to the total cost incurred by the producer of a good or service in order to create a profit. The total cost reflects the total amount of both fixed and variable expenses to produce and distribute a product.
   a. Price points
   b. Topics
   c. Premium pricing
   d. Markup

29. The _____ requires the Federal government to investigate and pursue trusts, companies and organizations suspected of violating the Act. It was the first United States Federal statute to limit cartels and monopolies, and today still forms the basis for most antitrust litigation by the federal government.
   a. 33 Strategies of War
   b. 28-hour day
   c. 1990 Clean Air Act
   d. Sherman Antitrust Act

30. _____, commonly known as e-commerce, consists of the buying and selling of products or services over electronic systems such as the Internet and other computer networks. The amount of trade conducted electronically has grown extraordinarily with widespread Internet usage. The use of commerce is conducted in this way, spurring and drawing on innovations in electronic funds transfer, supply chain management, Internet marketing, online transaction processing, electronic data interchange (EDI), inventory management systems, and automated data collection systems.
   a. Electronic Commerce
   b. A4e
   c. Online shopping
   d. A Stake in the Outcome

31. A _____ is typically described as a deliberate plan of action to guide decisions and achieve rational outcome(s.) However, the term may also be used to denote what is actually done, even though it is unplanned.

The term may apply to government, private sector organizations and groups, and individuals.

   a. 28-hour day
   b. 33 Strategies of War
   c. 1990 Clean Air Act
   d. Policy

32. Total _____ is a method of Accounting cost which entails the full cost of manufacturing or providing a service. This includes not just the costs of materials and labour, but also of all manufacturing overheads (whether 'fixed' or 'variable'.) One of the main reasons for absorbing overheads into the cost of units is for inventory valuation purposes.
   a. AAAI
   b. A Stake in the Outcome
   c. A4e
   d. Absorption costing

Chapter 8. Integrated Marketing Communications and Pricing Strategies

33. Why do retail stores need _____? With respect to the key objectives of growth and profit for any retail entity, _____ should significantly improve sales margins and increase sales by enabling the vendor to price variably and hence suitably and to control its product range based on profit margins. The retail stores will be able to compete more effectively with rivals in the form of mixed multiples, mail order and online retailers, who are often able to undercut but who do not generally have the same understanding of the retail market. In particular _____ is recognised as encouraging impulse buys, cross-selling of products and repeat sales.
   a. 28-hour day
   b. 1990 Clean Air Act
   c. Dynamic pricing
   d. 33 Strategies of War

34. _____ is a company's financial statement that indicates how the revenue is transformed into the net income The purpose of the _____ is to show managers and investors whether the company made or lost money during the period being reported.

The important thing to remember about an _____ is that it represents a period of time.

   a. AAAI
   b. A Stake in the Outcome
   c. Income statement
   d. A4e

35. A _____ is a process in which a potential employee is evaluated by an employer for prospective employment in their company, organization and was established in the late 16th century.

A _____ typically precedes the hiring decision, and is used to evaluate the candidate. The interview is usually preceded by the evaluation of submitted résumés from interested candidates, then selecting a small number of candidates for interviews.

   a. Split shift
   b. Supported employment
   c. Job interview
   d. Payrolling

36. In the English-speaking world, a _____ , also called a Member Service Provider is an outside company that is contracted by a member bank to procure new merchant relationships for the specific bank.
   a. A Stake in the Outcome
   b. A4e
   c. AAAI
   d. Independent sales organization

37. A _____ is a professional who provides advice in a particular area of expertise such as management, accountancy, the environment, entertainment, technology, law , human resources, marketing, medicine, finance, economics, public affairs, communication, engineering, sound system design, graphic design, or waste management.

A _____ is usually an expert or a professional in a specific field and has a wide knowledge of the subject matter. A _____ usually works for a consultancy firm or is self-employed, and engages with multiple and changing clients.

   a. 33 Strategies of War
   b. Consultant
   c. 1990 Clean Air Act
   d. 28-hour day

38. _____ exists when one firm provides goods or services to a customer with an agreement to bill them later, or receive a shipment or service from a supplier under an agreement to pay them later. It can be viewed as an essential element of capitalization in an operating business because it can reduce the required capital investment to operate the business if it is managed properly. _____ is the largest use of capital for a majority of business to business (B2B) sellers in the United States and is a critical source of capital for a majority of all businesses.
   a. 1990 Clean Air Act
   b. Trade credit
   c. Countertrade
   d. Buy-sell agreement

Chapter 9. Managing Cash Flow

1. _____ refers to the movement of cash into or out of a business or financial product. It is usually measured during a specified, finite period of time. Measurement of _____ can be used

   - to determine a project's rate of return or value. The time of _____s into and out of projects are used as inputs in financial models such as internal rate of return, and net present value.
   - to determine problems with a business's liquidity. Being profitable does not necessarily mean being liquid. A company can fail because of a shortage of cash, even while profitable.
   - as an alternate measure of a business's profits when it is believed that accrual accounting concepts do not represent economic realities. For example, a company may be notionally profitable but generating little operational cash (as may be the case for a company that barters its products rather than selling for cash.) In such a case, the company may be deriving additional operating cash by issuing shares evaluating default risk, re-investment requirements, etc.

   _____ is a generic term used differently depending on the context. It may be defined by users for their own purposes.

   a. Cash flow
   b. Gross profit margin
   c. Gross profit
   d. Sweat equity

2. In accounting, _____ or sales profit is the difference between revenue and the cost of making a product or providing a service, before deducting overhead, payroll, taxation, and interest payments. Note that this is different from operating profit (earnings before interest and taxes.)

   Net sales are calculated:

   Net sales = Sales - Sales returns and allowances.

   a. Capital budgeting
   b. Cash flow
   c. Gross profit margin
   d. Gross profit

3. _____ is a financial ratio used to assess the profitability of a firm's core activities, excluding fixed costs.

   The general calculation is:

   The _____ is related to the net profit margin, which assesses the profitability of an organization after including fixed costs.

   _____ indicates the relationship between net sales revenue and the cost of goods sold.

   a. Gross profit margin
   b. Sweat equity
   c. Capital structure
   d. Shareholder value

4. _____, net margin, net _____ or net profit ratio all refer to a measure of profitability. It is calculated by finding the net profit as a percentage of the revenue.

$$\text{Net profit margin} = \frac{\text{Net profit (after taxes)}}{\text{Revenue}} \times 100\%$$

The _____ is mostly used for internal comparison.

a. 1990 Clean Air Act
b. Profit maximization
c. Net profit margin
d. Profit margin

5. An _____ is a person who has possession of an enterprise and assumes significant accountability for the inherent risks and the outcome. It is an ambitious leader who combines land, labor, and capital to create and market new goods or services. The term is a loanword from French and was first defined by the Irish economist Richard Cantillon.

a. Entrepreneur
b. A4e
c. A Stake in the Outcome
d. AAAI

6. _____ generally refers to a list of all planned expenses and revenues. It is a plan for saving and spending. A _____ is an important concept in microeconomics, which uses a _____ line to illustrate the trade-offs between two or more goods.

a. 1990 Clean Air Act
b. 33 Strategies of War
c. 28-hour day
d. Budget

7. _____ is the process of estimation in unknown situations. Prediction is a similar, but more general term. Both can refer to estimation of time series, cross-sectional or longitudinal data.

a. 1990 Clean Air Act
b. 33 Strategies of War
c. 28-hour day
d. Forecasting

8. Marketing research is a form of business research and is generally divided into two categories: consumer _____ and business-to-business (B2B) _____, which was previously known as industrial marketing research. Consumer marketing research studies the buying habits of individual people while business-to-business marketing research investigates the markets for products sold by one business to another.

Consumer _____ is a form of applied sociology that concentrates on understanding the behaviours, whims and preferences, of consumers in a market-based economy, and aims to understand the effects and comparative success of marketing campaigns.

a. Mystery shoppers
b. Questionnaire construction
c. Questionnaire
d. Market research

9. A _____ is a formal statement of a set of business goals, the reasons why they are believed attainable, and the plan for reaching those goals. It may also contain background information about the organization or team attempting to reach those goals.

The business goals may be defined for for-profit or for non-profit organizations.

a. Time management
b. Distributed management
c. Crisis management
d. Business plan

10. _____ is one of a series of accounting transactions dealing with the billing of customers who owe money to a person, company or organization for goods and services that have been provided to the customer. In most business entities this is typically done by generating an invoice and mailing or electronically delivering it to the customer, who in turn must pay it within an established timeframe called credit or payment terms.

An example of a common payment term is Net 30, meaning payment is due in the amount of the invoice 30 days from the date of invoice.

a. Accumulated Depreciation
b. Other revenue
c. A Stake in the Outcome
d. Accounts receivable

11. A _____ is a business that is privately owned and operated, with a small number of employees and relatively low volume of sales. The legal definition of 'small' often varies by country and industry, but is generally under 100 employees in the United States and under 50 employees in the European Union. In comparison, the definition of mid-sized business by the number of employees is generally under 500 in the U.S. and 250 for the European Union.

a. Small Business
b. Pre-determined overhead rate
c. Golden Boot Compensation
d. Critical Success Factor

12. A _____ is typically described as a deliberate plan of action to guide decisions and achieve rational outcome(s). However, the term may also be used to denote what is actually done, even though it is unplanned.

The term may apply to government, private sector organizations and groups, and individuals.

a. 28-hour day
b. 33 Strategies of War
c. 1990 Clean Air Act
d. Policy

13. In physics, and more specifically kinematics, _____ is the change in velocity over time. Because velocity is a vector, it can change in two ways: a change in magnitude and/or a change in direction. In one dimension, _____ is the rate at which something speeds up or slows down.

a. AAAI
b. Acceleration
c. A Stake in the Outcome
d. A4e

14. In economics, business, retail, and accounting, a _____ is the value of money that has been used up to produce something, and hence is not available for use anymore. In economics, a _____ is an alternative that is given up as a result of a decision. In business, the _____ may be one of acquisition, in which case the amount of money expended to acquire it is counted as _____.

a. Fixed costs
b. Cost allocation
c. Cost overrun
d. Cost

15. A _____ is a relatively new executive level position at a corporation, company, organization typically reporting directly to the CEO or board of directors. The _____ is responsible for a brand's image, experience, and promise, and propagating it throughout all aspects of the company. The brand officer oversees marketing, advertising, design, public relations and customer service departments.

a. Chief brand officer
b. Director of communications
c. Purchasing manager
d. Chief executive officer

16. _____ is one of the four Ps of the marketing mix. The other three aspects are product, promotion, and place. It is also a key variable in microeconomic price allocation theory.
   a. Pricing
   b. Price floor
   c. Transfer pricing
   d. Penetration pricing

17. _____ is a file or account that contains money that a person or company owes to suppliers, but has not paid yet (a form of debt.) When you receive an invoice you add it to the file, and then you remove it when you pay. Thus, the A/P is a form of credit that suppliers offer to their purchasers by allowing them to pay for a product or service after it has already been received.
   a. Other revenue
   b. Accounts payable
   c. A Stake in the Outcome
   d. Accounts receivable

18. The _____, first published in 1952, is one of a number of uniform acts that have been promulgated in conjunction with efforts to harmonize the law of sales and other commercial transactions in all 50 states within the United States of America. This objective is deemed important because of the prevalence of commercial transactions that extend beyond one state (for example, where the goods are manufactured in state A, warehoused in state B, sold from state C and delivered in state D.) The _____ deals primarily with transactions involving personal property (movable property), not real property (immovable property.)
   a. A Stake in the Outcome
   b. Uniform Commercial Code
   c. A4e
   d. AAAI

19. In a human resources context, _____ or labor _____ is the rate at which an employer gains and loses employees. Simple ways to describe it are 'how long employees tend to stay' or 'the rate of traffic through the revolving door.' _____ is measured for individual companies and for their industry as a whole. If an employer is said to have a high _____ relative to its competitors, it means that employees of that company have a shorter average tenure than those of other companies in the same industry.
   a. Ten year occupational employment projection
   b. Continuous
   c. Career portfolios
   d. Turnover

20. _____ is a form of communication that typically attempts to persuade potential customers to purchase or to consume more of a particular brand of product or service. 'While now central to the contemporary global economy and the reproduction of global production networks, it is only quite recently that _____ has been more than a marginal influence on patterns of sales and production. The formation of modern _____ was intimately bound up with the emergence of new forms of monopoly capitalism around the end of the 19th and beginning of the 20th century as one element in corporate strategies to create, organize and where possible control markets, especially for mass produced consumer goods.
   a. A4e
   b. AAAI
   c. Advertising
   d. A Stake in the Outcome

21. _____ is a financial metric which represents operating liquidity available to a business. Along with fixed assets such as plant and equipment, _____ is considered a part of operating capital. It is calculated as current assets minus current liabilities.

Chapter 9. Managing Cash Flow

a. 1990 Clean Air Act
b. 33 Strategies of War
c. 28-hour day
d. Working capital

22. In finance, a _____ or accounting ratio is a ratio of two selected numerical values taken from an enterprise's financial statements. There are many standard ratios used to try to evaluate the overall financial condition of a corporation or other organization. _____s may be used by managers within a firm, by current and potential shareholders (owners) of a firm, and by a firm's creditors.

a. Financial Ratio
b. Return on equity
c. Return on sales
d. Rate of return

23. _____ is exchange of capital, goods, and services across international borders or territories. In most countries, it represents a significant share of gross domestic product (GDP.) While _____ has been present throughout much of history, its economic, social, and political importance has been on the rise in recent centuries.

a. A4e
b. AAAI
c. International Trade
d. A Stake in the Outcome

24. In business, overhead, _____ or overhead expense refers to an ongoing expense of operating a business. The term overhead is usually used to group expenses that are necessary to the continued functioning of the business, but do not directly generate profits.

Overhead expenses are all costs on the income statement except for direct labor and direct materials.

a. Industrial market segmentation
b. Overhead cost
c. Intangible assets
d. Interlocking directorate

25. _____ is a technique of planning and decision-making which reverses the working process of traditional budgeting. In traditional incremental budgeting, departmental managers justify only increases over the previous year budget and what has been already spent is automatically sanctioned. No reference is made to the previous level of expenditure.

a. 33 Strategies of War
b. 28-hour day
c. 1990 Clean Air Act
d. Zero-based budgeting

Chapter 10. Creating a Successful Financial Plan

1. In business and accounting, _____s are everything of value that is owned by a person or company. Any property or object of value that one possesses, usually considered as applicable to the payment of one's debts is considered an _____. Simplistically stated, _____s are things of value that can be readily converted into cash.
   a. AAAI
   b. A4e
   c. A Stake in the Outcome
   d. Asset

2. In financial accounting, a _____ or statement of financial position is a summary of a person's or organization's balances. Assets, liabilities and ownership equity are listed as of a specific date, such as the end of its financial year. A _____ is often described as a snapshot of a company's financial condition.
   a. 33 Strategies of War
   b. Balance sheet
   c. 1990 Clean Air Act
   d. 28-hour day

3. In accounting, a _____ is an asset on the balance sheet which is expected to be sold or otherwise used up in the near future, usually within one year, or one business cycle - whichever is longer. Typical _____s include cash, cash equivalents, accounts receivable, inventory, the portion of prepaid accounts which will be used within a year, and short-term investments.

   On the balance sheet, assets will typically be classified into _____s and long-term assets.

   a. Net income
   b. Current asset
   c. Treasury stock
   d. Matching principle

4. In finance, _____ are considered liabilities of the business that are to be settled in cash within the fiscal year or the operating cycle, whichever period is longer.

   For example accounts payable for goods, services or supplies that were purchased for use in the operation of the business and payable within a normal period of time would be _____.

   Bonds, mortgages and loans that are payable over a term exceeding one year would be fixed liabilities.

   a. Generally accepted accounting principles
   b. Depreciation
   c. Current liabilities
   d. Matching principle

5. _____ are formal records of the financial activities of a business, person, or other entity. In British English, including United Kingdom company law, _____ are often referred to as accounts, although the term _____ is also used, particularly by accountants.

   _____ provide an overview of a business or person's financial condition in both short and long term.

   a. 33 Strategies of War
   b. 1990 Clean Air Act
   c. 28-hour day
   d. Financial statements

6. _____ plant, and equipment, is a term used in accountancy for assets and property which cannot easily be converted into cash. This can be compared with current assets such as cash or bank accounts, which are described as liquid assets. In most cases, only tangible assets are referred to as fixed.

a. 33 Strategies of War
c. 1990 Clean Air Act
b. 28-hour day
d. Fixed asset

7. In economics, business, retail, and accounting, a _____ is the value of money that has been used up to produce something, and hence is not available for use anymore. In economics, a _____ is an alternative that is given up as a result of a decision. In business, the _____ may be one of acquisition, in which case the amount of money expended to acquire it is counted as _____.

a. Cost allocation
c. Fixed costs
b. Cost overrun
d. Cost

8. In financial accounting, _____ or cost of sales includes the direct costs attributable to the production of the goods sold by a company. This amount includes the materials cost used in creating the goods along with the direct labour costs used to produce the good. It excludes indirect expenses such as distribution costs and sales force costs.

a. 1990 Clean Air Act
c. 28-hour day
b. Reorder point
d. Cost of goods sold

9. _____ is a company's financial statement that indicates how the revenue is transformed into the net income The purpose of the _____ is to show managers and investors whether the company made or lost money during the period being reported.

The important thing to remember about an _____ is that it represents a period of time.

a. AAAI
c. A Stake in the Outcome
b. A4e
d. Income statement

10. In accounting, _____ or sales profit is the difference between revenue and the cost of making a product or providing a service, before deducting overhead, payroll, taxation, and interest payments. Note that this is different from operating profit (earnings before interest and taxes.)

Net sales are calculated:

Net sales = Sales - Sales returns and allowances.

a. Cash flow
c. Gross profit margin
b. Capital budgeting
d. Gross profit

11. _____ is a financial ratio used to assess the profitability of a firm's core activities, excluding fixed costs.

The general calculation is:

The _____ is related to the net profit margin, which assesses the profitability of an organization after including fixed costs.

Chapter 10. Creating a Successful Financial Plan

_____ indicates the relationship between net sales revenue and the cost of goods sold.

a. Sweat equity
c. Shareholder value
b. Capital structure
d. Gross profit margin

12. An _____, operating expenditure, operational expense, operational expenditure or OPEX is an on-going cost for running a product, business, or system. Its counterpart, a capital expenditure (CAPEX), is the cost of developing or providing non-consumable parts for the product or system. For example, the purchase of a photocopier is the CAPEX, and the annual paper and toner cost is the OPEX.

a. Operating expense
c. A Stake in the Outcome
b. AAAI
d. A4e

13. _____, net margin, net _____ or net profit ratio all refer to a measure of profitability. It is calculated by finding the net profit as a percentage of the revenue.

$$\text{Net profit margin} = \frac{\text{Net profit (after taxes)}}{\text{Revenue}} \times 100\%$$

The _____ is mostly used for internal comparison.

a. 1990 Clean Air Act
c. Profit margin
b. Net profit margin
d. Profit maximization

14. In financial accounting, a cash flow statement or _____ is a financial statement that shows how changes in balance sheet and income accounts affect cash and cash equivalents, and breaks the analysis down to operating, investing, and financing activities. As an analytical tool, the _____ is useful in determining the short-term viability of a company, particularly its ability to pay bills. International Accounting Standard 7 (IAS 7), is the International Accounting Standard that deals with cash flow statements.

a. Statement of cash flows
c. 1990 Clean Air Act
b. 33 Strategies of War
d. 28-hour day

15. _____ refers to the movement of cash into or out of a business or financial product. It is usually measured during a specified, finite period of time. Measurement of _____ can be used

- to determine a project's rate of return or value. The time of _____s into and out of projects are used as inputs in financial models such as internal rate of return, and net present value.
- to determine problems with a business's liquidity. Being profitable does not necessarily mean being liquid. A company can fail because of a shortage of cash, even while profitable.
- as an alternate measure of a business's profits when it is believed that accrual accounting concepts do not represent economic realities. For example, a company may be notionally profitable but generating little operational cash (as may be the case for a company that barters its products rather than selling for cash.) In such a case, the company may be deriving additional operating cash by issuing shares evaluating default risk, re-investment requirements, etc.

_____ is a generic term used differently depending on the context. It may be defined by users for their own purposes.

a. Sweat equity
b. Cash flow
c. Gross profit
d. Gross profit margin

16. The _____ of an edge is $c_f(u,v) = c(u,v) - f(u,v)$. This defines a residual network denoted $G_f(V, E_f)$, giving the amount of available capacity. See that there can be an edge from u to v in the residual network, even though there is no edge from u to v in the original network.

a. 1990 Clean Air Act
b. Residual capacity
c. 28-hour day
d. 33 Strategies of War

17. A _____ is a business that is privately owned and operated, with a small number of employees and relatively low volume of sales. The legal definition of 'small' often varies by country and industry, but is generally under 100 employees in the United States and under 50 employees in the European Union. In comparison, the definition of mid-sized business by the number of employees is generally under 500 in the U.S. and 250 for the European Union.

a. Critical Success Factor
b. Pre-determined overhead rate
c. Golden Boot Compensation
d. Small business

18. In finance, the _____ or quick ratio or liquid ratio measures the ability of a company to use its near cash or quick assets to immediately extinguish or retire its current liabilities. Quick assets include those current assets that presumably can be quickly converted to cash at close to their book values.

Generally, the acid test ratio should be 1:1 or better, however this varies widely by industry.

a. A4e
b. Inventory turnover
c. A Stake in the Outcome
d. Acid-test

19. The _____ is a financial ratio that measures whether or not a firm has enough resources to pay its debts over the next 12 months. It compares a firm's current assets to its current liabilities. It is expressed as follows:

$$\text{Current ratio} = \frac{\text{Current Assets}}{\text{Current Liabilities}}$$

For example, if WXY Company's current assets are $50,000,000 and its current liabilities are $40,000,000, then its _____ would be $50,000,000 divided by $40,000,000, which equals 1.25.

a. Return on assets
b. Times interest earned
c. Financial ratio
d. Current ratio

20. Market _____ is a business, economics or investment term that refers to an asset's ability to be easily converted through an act of buying or selling without causing a significant movement in the price and with minimum loss of value. Money, or cash on hand, is the most liquid asset. An act of exchange of a less liquid asset with a more liquid asset is called liquidation.

Chapter 10. Creating a Successful Financial Plan

a. 28-hour day
c. 33 Strategies of War
b. 1990 Clean Air Act
d. Liquidity

21. _____ is a financial metric which represents operating liquidity available to a business. Along with fixed assets such as plant and equipment, _____ is considered a part of operating capital. It is calculated as current assets minus current liabilities.

a. 33 Strategies of War
c. 28-hour day
b. 1990 Clean Air Act
d. Working capital

22. _____ is a financial ratio that indicates the percentage of a company's assets are provided via debt. It is the ratio of total debt (the sum of current liabilities and long-term liabilities) and total assets (the sum of current assets, fixed assets, and other assets such as 'goodwill'.)

$$\text{Debt ratio} = \frac{\text{Total Debt}}{\text{Total Assets}}$$

or alternatively:

$$\text{Debt ratio} = \frac{\text{Total Liability}}{\text{Total Assets}}$$

For example, a company with $2 million in total assets and $500,000 in total liabilities would have a _____ of 25%

Like all financial ratios, a company's _____ should be compared with their industry average or other competing firms.

a. 1990 Clean Air Act
c. Debt ratio
b. Demand forecasting
d. 28-hour day

23. In finance, _____ is borrowing money to supplement existing funds for investment in such a way that the potential positive or negative outcome is magnified and/or enhanced. It generally refers to using borrowed funds, or debt, so as to attempt to increase the returns to equity. Deleveraging is the action of reducing borrowings.

a. Private equity
c. Limited liability corporation
b. Gearing
d. Limited partners

24. _____ is a measure of a company's earning power from ongoing operations, equal to earnings before the deduction of interest payments and income taxes.

To accountants, economic profit, or EP, is a single-period metric to determine the value created by a company in one period - usually a year. It is the net profit after tax less the equity charge, a risk-weighted cost of capital.

a. Operating profit
c. AAAI
b. A4e
d. A Stake in the Outcome

25. _____ or interest coverage ratio is a measure of a company's ability to honor its debt payments. It may be calculated as either EBIT or EBITDA divided by the total interest payable.

a. Return on sales
b. Rate of return
c. P/E ratio
d. Times interest earned

26. In business, _____ is the total liabilities minus total outside assets of an individual or a company. For a company, this is called shareholders' preference and may be referred to as book value. _____ is stated as at a particular year in time.

a. Novated lease
b. Net worth
c. Payback period
d. Deferred compensation

27. The _____ is a financial term defined as a company's operating expenses as a percentage of revenue. This financial ratio is most commonly used for industries such as railroads which require a large percentage of revenues to maintain operations. In railroading, an _____ of 80 or lower is considered desirable.

a. A4e
b. A Stake in the Outcome
c. AAAI
d. Operating ratio

28. The _____ is an equation that equals the cost of goods sold divided by the average inventory. Average inventory equals beginning inventory plus ending inventory divided by 2.

The formula for _____:

The formula for average inventory:

A low turnover rate may point to overstocking, obsolescence, or deficiencies in the product line or marketing effort.

a. Inventory turnover
b. A Stake in the Outcome
c. A4e
d. Asset turnover

29. _____ is one of the Accounting Liquidity ratios, a financial ratio. This ratio measures the number of times, on average, the inventory is sold during the period. Its purpose is to measure the liquidity of the inventory.

a. Inventory turnover ratio
b. A Stake in the Outcome
c. Inventory
d. A4e

30. In a human resources context, _____ or labor _____ is the rate at which an employer gains and loses employees. Simple ways to describe it are 'how long employees tend to stay' or 'the rate of traffic through the revolving door.' _____ is measured for individual companies and for their industry as a whole. If an employer is said to have a high _____ relative to its competitors, it means that employees of that company have a shorter average tenure than those of other companies in the same industry.

a. Continuous
b. Ten year occupational employment projection
c. Career portfolios
d. Turnover

31. _____ is a financial ratio that measures the efficiency of a company's use of its assets in generating sales revenue or sales income to the company.

$$Asset\ Turnover = \frac{Sales}{Average Total Assets}$$

- 'Sales' is the value of 'Net Sales' or 'Sales' from the company's income statement
- 'Average Total Assets' is the value of 'Total assets' from the company's balance sheet in the beginning and the end of the fiscal period divided by 2.

a. Inventory turnover
b. Asset turnover
c. A4e
d. A Stake in the Outcome

32. _____ is the process of estimation in unknown situations. Prediction is a similar, but more general term. Both can refer to estimation of time series, cross-sectional or longitudinal data.

a. 1990 Clean Air Act
b. 28-hour day
c. 33 Strategies of War
d. Forecasting

33. In business and finance accounting, _____ is equal to the gross profit minus overheads minus interest payable plus/minus one off items for a given time period (usually: accounting period.)

A common synonym for '_____' when discussing financial statements (which include a balance sheet and an income statement) is the bottom line. This term results from the traditional appearance of an income statement which shows all allocated revenues and expenses over a specified time period with the resulting summation on the bottom line of the report.

a. Generally accepted accounting principles
b. Matching principle
c. Treasury stock
d. Net profit

34. Profit margin, net margin, _____ or net profit ratio all refer to a measure of profitability. It is calculated by finding the net profit as a percentage of the revenue.

The profit margin is mostly used for internal comparison.

Chapter 10. Creating a Successful Financial Plan

a. 1990 Clean Air Act
b. Net profit margin
c. Profit maximization
d. Profit margin

35. The _____ is a measure of how revenue growth translates into growth in operating income. It is a measure of leverage, and of how risky (volatile) a company's operating income is.

There are various measures of _____, which can be interpreted analogously to financial leverage.

a. A4e
b. A Stake in the Outcome
c. Operating leverage
d. AAAI

36. _____ refers to the methods of practicing and using another person's business philosophy. The franchisor grants the independent operator the right to distribute its products, techniques, and trademarks for a percentage of gross monthly sales and a royalty fee. Various tangibles and intangibles such as national or international advertising, training, and other support services are commonly made available by the franchisor.

a. 1990 Clean Air Act
b. Franchising
c. 28-hour day
d. ServiceMaster

37. _____ is a mathematical science pertaining to the collection, analysis, interpretation or explanation, and presentation of data. It also provides tools for prediction and forecasting based on data. It is applicable to a wide variety of academic disciplines, from the natural and social sciences to the humanities, government and business.

a. Location parameter
b. Simple moving average
c. Failure rate
d. Statistics

38. The _____ is an independent agency of the United States government, established in 1914 by the _____ Act. Its principal mission is the promotion of 'consumer protection' and the elimination and prevention of what regulators perceive to be harmfully 'anti-competitive' business practices, such as coercive monopoly.

The _____ Act was one of President Wilson's major acts against trusts.

a. 28-hour day
b. Federal Trade Commission
c. 1990 Clean Air Act
d. 33 Strategies of War

39. In finance, a _____ or accounting ratio is a ratio of two selected numerical values taken from an enterprise's financial statements. There are many standard ratios used to try to evaluate the overall financial condition of a corporation or other organization. _____s may be used by managers within a firm, by current and potential shareholders (owners) of a firm, and by a firm's creditors.

a. Return on sales
b. Return on equity
c. Rate of return
d. Financial Ratio

40. An _____ is an organization founded and funded by businesses that operate in a specific industry. An industry trade association participates in public relations activities such as advertising, education, political donations, lobbying and publishing, but its main focus is collaboration between companies, or standardization. Associations may offer other services, such as producing conferences, networking or charitable events or offering classes or educational materials.

a. A Stake in the Outcome
b. Industry trade group
c. AAAI
d. A4e

41. In economics ' business, specifically cost accounting, the _____ is the point at which cost or expenses and revenue are equal: there is no net loss or gain, and one has 'broken even'. A profit or a loss has not been made, although opportunity costs have been paid, and capital has received the risk-adjusted, expected return.

For example, if the business sells less than 200 tables each month, it will make a loss, if it sells more, it will be a profit.

a. Fixed asset turnover
b. Virtuous circle
c. Defined benefit pension plan
d. Break-even point

Chapter 11. Crafting a Winning Business Plan

1. A _____ is a formal statement of a set of business goals, the reasons why they are believed attainable, and the plan for reaching those goals. It may also contain background information about the organization or team attempting to reach those goals.

The business goals may be defined for for-profit or for non-profit organizations.

   a. Time management
   c. Distributed management
   b. Crisis management
   d. Business plan

2. A _____ is a list of the general tasks and responsibilities of a position. Typically, it also includes to whom the position reports, specifications such as the qualifications needed by the person in the job, salary range for the position, etc. A _____ is usually developed by conducting a job analysis, which includes examining the tasks and sequences of tasks necessary to perform the job.
   a. Recruitment advertising
   c. Recruitment Process Insourcing
   b. Recruitment
   d. Job description

3. A _____ is a business that is privately owned and operated, with a small number of employees and relatively low volume of sales. The legal definition of 'small' often varies by country and industry, but is generally under 100 employees in the United States and under 50 employees in the European Union. In comparison, the definition of mid-sized business by the number of employees is generally under 500 in the U.S. and 250 for the European Union.
   a. Small Business
   c. Pre-determined overhead rate
   b. Golden Boot Compensation
   d. Critical Success Factor

4. The _____ is a United States government agency that provides support to small businesses.

The mission of the _____ is 'to maintain and strengthen the nation's economy by enabling the establishment and viability of small businesses and by assisting in the economic recovery of communities after disasters.'

The _____ makes loans directly to businesses and acts as a guarantor on bank loans. In some circumstances it also makes loans to victims of natural disasters, works to get government procurement contracts for small businesses, and assists businesses with management, technical and training issues.

   a. Small Business Administration
   c. 28-hour day
   b. 1990 Clean Air Act
   d. 33 Strategies of War

5. A _____ is a brief written statement of the purpose of a company or organization. Ideally, a _____ guides the actions of the organization, spells out its overall goal, provides a sense of direction, and guides decision making for all levels of management.

_____s often contain the following:

- Purpose and aim of the organization
- The organization's primary stakeholders: clients, stockholders, etc.
- Responsibilities of the organization toward these stakeholders
- Products and services offered

Chapter 11. Crafting a Winning Business Plan

In developing a _____:

- Encourage as much input as feasible from employees, volunteers, and other stakeholders
- Publicize it broadly

The _____ can be used to resolve differences between business stakeholders. Stakeholders include: employees including managers and executives, stockholders, board of directors, customers, suppliers, distributors, creditors, governments (local, state, federal, etc.), unions, competitors, NGO's, and the general public.

a. 33 Strategies of War
c. Mission statement
b. 1990 Clean Air Act
d. 28-hour day

6. _____ refers to the aggregated strategies of single business firm or a strategic business unit (SBU) in a diversified corporation. According to Michael Porter, a firm must formulate a _____ that incorporates either cost leadership, differentiation or focus in order to achieve a sustainable competitive advantage and long-term success in its chosen arenas or industries.

Functional strategies include marketing strategies, new product development strategies, human resource strategies, financial strategies, legal strategies, supply-chain strategies, and information technology management strategies.

a. Strategic thinking
c. Switching cost
b. Competitive heterogeneity
d. Business strategy

7. _____ refers to the movement of cash into or out of a business or financial product. It is usually measured during a specified, finite period of time. Measurement of _____ can be used

- to determine a project's rate of return or value. The time of _____s into and out of projects are used as inputs in financial models such as internal rate of return, and net present value.
- to determine problems with a business's liquidity. Being profitable does not necessarily mean being liquid. A company can fail because of a shortage of cash, even while profitable.
- as an alternate measure of a business's profits when it is believed that accrual accounting concepts do not represent economic realities. For example, a company may be notionally profitable but generating little operational cash (as may be the case for a company that barters its products rather than selling for cash.) In such a case, the company may be deriving additional operating cash by issuing shares evaluating default risk, re-investment requirements, etc.

_____ is a generic term used differently depending on the context. It may be defined by users for their own purposes.

a. Gross profit margin
c. Sweat equity
b. Gross profit
d. Cash flow

Chapter 11. Crafting a Winning Business Plan

8. _____ is an integrated communications-based process through which individuals and communities discover that existing and newly-identified needs and wants may be satisfied by the products and services of others.

_____ is defined by the American _____ Association as the activity, set of institutions, and processes for creating, communicating, delivering, and exchanging offerings that have value for customers, clients, partners, and society at large. The term developed from the original meaning which referred literally to going to market, as in shopping, or going to a market to buy or sell goods or services.

a. Marketing
b. Market development
c. Customer relationship management
d. Disruptive technology

9. A _____ is a process that can allow an organization to concentrate its limited resources on the greatest opportunities to increase sales and achieve a sustainable competitive advantage. A _____ should be centered around the key concept that customer satisfaction is the main goal.

A _____ is a written plan which combines product development, promotion, distribution, and pricing approach, identifies the firm's marketing goals, and explains how they will be achieved within a stated timeframe.

a. Category management
b. Disruptive technology
c. Product bundling
d. Marketing strategy

10. _____ is a form of communication that typically attempts to persuade potential customers to purchase or to consume more of a particular brand of product or service. 'While now central to the contemporary global economy and the reproduction of global production networks, it is only quite recently that _____ has been more than a marginal influence on patterns of sales and production. The formation of modern _____ was intimately bound up with the emergence of new forms of monopoly capitalism around the end of the 19th and beginning of the 20th century as one element in corporate strategies to create, organize and where possible control markets, especially for mass produced consumer goods.

a. A4e
b. Advertising
c. AAAI
d. A Stake in the Outcome

11. A _____ is a documented investigation of a Market that is used to inform a firm's planning activities particularly around decision of: inventory, purchase, work force expansion/contraction, facility expansion, purchases of capital equipment, promotional activities, and many other aspects of a company.

Not all managers are asked to conduct a _____, but all managers must make decisions using _____ data and understand how the data was derived. So all managers need a reasonable understanding of the tools most used for making sales forecasts and analyzing markets.

a. Market analysis
b. Marketing research
c. 1990 Clean Air Act
d. Marketing research process

12. _____ is an idea in the field of Organizational studies and management which describes the psychology, attitudes, experiences, beliefs and Values (personal and cultural values) of an organization. It has been defined as 'the specific collection of values and norms that are shared by people and groups in an organization and that control the way they interact with each other and with stakeholders outside the organization.'

Chapter 11. Crafting a Winning Business Plan

This definition continues to explain organizational values also known as 'beliefs and ideas about what kinds of goals members of an organization should pursue and ideas about the appropriate kinds or standards of behavior organizational members should use to achieve these goals. From organizational values develop organizational norms, guidelines or expectations that prescribe appropriate kinds of behavior by employees in particular situations and control the behavior of organizational members towards one another.'

_____ is not the same as corporate culture.

a. Organizational effectiveness
b. Organizational development
c. Union shop
d. Organizational culture

13. _____ is one of the four Ps of the marketing mix. The other three aspects are product, promotion, and place. It is also a key variable in microeconomic price allocation theory.
a. Pricing
b. Price floor
c. Transfer pricing
d. Penetration pricing

14. The term '_____' refers to the concept of collecting information and attempting to spot a pattern in the information. In some fields of study, the term '_____' has more formally-defined meanings.

In project management _____ is a mathematical technique that uses historical results to predict future outcome.

a. Stepwise regression
b. Least squares
c. Regression analysis
d. Trend analysis

15. _____ is one of the four elements of marketing mix. An organization or set of organizations (go-betweens) involved in the process of making a product or service available for use or consumption by a consumer or business user.

The other three parts of the marketing mix are product, pricing, and promotion.

a. Job creation programs
b. Matching theory
c. Missing completely at random
d. Distribution

16. _____ in marketing and strategic management is an assessment of the strengths and weaknesses of current and potential competitors. This analysis provides both an offensive and defensive strategic context through which to identify opportunities and threats. Competitor profiling coalesces all of the relevant sources of _____ into one framework in the support of efficient and effective strategy formulation, implementation, monitoring and adjustment.
a. Competitor or Competitive Intelligence
b. 28-hour day
c. Competitor analysis
d. 1990 Clean Air Act

17. A _____ is directly responsible for managing the day-to-day operations (and profitability) of a company.

Chief Executive Officer (CEO)
- As the top manager, the CEO is typically responsible for the entire operations of the corporation and reports directly to the chairman and board of directors. It is the CEO's responsibility to implement board decisions and initiatives and to maintain the smooth operation of the firm, with the assistance of senior management.

   a. Vorstand   b. Field service management
   c. Getting Things Done   d. Management team

18. A _____ is an entity formed between two or more parties to undertake economic activity together. The parties agree to create a new entity by both contributing equity, and they then share in the revenues, expenses, and control of the enterprise. The venture can be for one specific project only, or a continuing business relationship such as the Fuji Xerox _____.

   a. Joint venture   b. Patent
   c. Meritor Savings Bank v. Vinson   d. Civil Rights Act of 1991

19. _____ is a concept whereby a person's financial liability is limited to a fixed sum, most commonly the value of a person's investment in a company or partnership with _____. In other words, if a company with _____ is sued, then the plaintiffs are suing the company, not its owners or investors. A shareholder in a limited company is not personally liable for any of the debts of the company, other than for the value of his investment in that company.

   a. Partnership   b. Toxic Substances Control Act
   c. Privity   d. Limited liability

20. A _____ in the law of the vast majority of United States jurisdictions is a legal form of business company that provides limited liability to its owners. Often incorrectly called a 'limited liability corporation' (instead of company), it is a hybrid business entity having certain characteristics of both a corporation and a partnership or sole proprietorship (depending on how many owners there are.) The primary characteristic an _____ shares with a corporation is limited liability, and the primary characteristic it shares with a partnership is the availability of pass-through income taxation.

   a. Limited partners   b. Growth capital
   c. Limited liability company   d. Venture Capitalist

21. A _____ is a type of business entity in which partners (owners) share with each other the profits or losses of the business. _____s are often favored over corporations for taxation purposes, as the _____ structure does not generally incur a tax on profits before it is distributed to the partners (i.e. there is no dividend tax levied.) However, depending on the _____ structure and the jurisdiction in which it operates, owners of a _____ may be exposed to greater personal liability than they would as shareholders of a corporation.

   a. Federal Employers Liability Act   b. Due process
   c. Mediation   d. Partnership

22. An _____, for United States federal income tax purposes, is a corporation that makes a valid election to be taxed under Subchapter S of Chapter 1 of the Internal Revenue Code.

In general, _____s do not pay any income taxes. Instead, the corporation's income or losses are divided among and passed through to its shareholders.

Chapter 11. Crafting a Winning Business Plan

a. 28-hour day
b. 33 Strategies of War
c. 1990 Clean Air Act
d. S corporation

23. _____ are formal records of the financial activities of a business, person, or other entity. In British English, including United Kingdom company law, _____ are often referred to as accounts, although the term _____ is also used, particularly by accountants.

_____ provide an overview of a business or person's financial condition in both short and long term.

a. 1990 Clean Air Act
b. 28-hour day
c. 33 Strategies of War
d. Financial statements

24. An _____ is a person who has possession of an enterprise and assumes significant accountability for the inherent risks and the outcome. It is an ambitious leader who combines land, labor, and capital to create and market new goods or services. The term is a loanword from French and was first defined by the Irish economist Richard Cantillon.

a. A Stake in the Outcome
b. A4e
c. AAAI
d. Entrepreneur

25. An _____ is any party that makes an investment.

The term has taken on a specific meaning in finance to describe the particular types of people and companies that regularly purchase equity or debt securities for financial gain in exchange for funding an expanding company. Less frequently, the term is applied to parties who purchase real estate, currency, commodity derivatives, personal property, or other assets.

a. A4e
b. AAAI
c. A Stake in the Outcome
d. Investor

26. _____ is a type of private equity capital typically provided to early-stage, high-potential, growth companies in the interest of generating a return through an eventual realization event such as an IPO or trade sale of the company. _____ investments are generally made as cash in exchange for shares in the invested company. It is typical for _____ investors to identify and back companies in high technology industries such as biotechnology and ICT.

a. Private equity
b. Limited liability corporation
c. Venture Capital
d. Seed round

27. A _____ is a set of exclusive rights granted by a state to an inventor or his assignee for a limited period of time in exchange for a disclosure of an invention.

The procedure for granting _____s, the requirements placed on the _____ee and the extent of the exclusive rights vary widely between countries according to national laws and international agreements. Typically, however, a _____ application must include one or more claims defining the invention which must be new, inventive, and useful or industrially applicable.

a. Patent
b. Labor Management Reporting and Disclosure Act
c. Food, Drug, and Cosmetic Act
d. Federal Trade Commission Act

28. _____ is a strategic planning method used to evaluate the Strengths, Weaknesses, Opportunities, and Threats involved in a project or in a business venture. It involves specifying the objective of the business venture or project and identifying the internal and external factors that are favorable and unfavorable to achieving that objective. The technique is credited to Albert Humphrey, who led a convention at Stanford University in the 1960s and 1970s using data from Fortune 500 companies.

a. Corporate image
b. SWOT analysis
c. Marketing
d. Market share

29. A _____ is a distinctive sign or indicator used by an individual, business organization, or other legal entity to identify that the products and/or services to consumers with which the _____ appears originate from a unique source and to distinguish its products or services from those of other entities.

a. Trademark
b. Succession planning
c. Virtual team
d. Kanban

30. In business and accounting, _____s are everything of value that is owned by a person or company. Any property or object of value that one possesses, usually considered as applicable to the payment of one's debts is considered an _____. Simplistically stated, _____s are things of value that can be readily converted into cash.

a. A4e
b. AAAI
c. Asset
d. A Stake in the Outcome

31. In financial accounting, a _____ or statement of financial position is a summary of a person's or organization's balances. Assets, liabilities and ownership equity are listed as of a specific date, such as the end of its financial year. A _____ is often described as a snapshot of a company's financial condition.

a. 28-hour day
b. Balance sheet
c. 1990 Clean Air Act
d. 33 Strategies of War

32. _____ is a company's financial statement that indicates how the revenue is transformed into the net income The purpose of the _____ is to show managers and investors whether the company made or lost money during the period being reported.

The important thing to remember about an _____ is that it represents a period of time.

a. A Stake in the Outcome
b. AAAI
c. A4e
d. Income statement

Chapter 12. Sources of Financing: Debt and Equity

1. In business and accounting, _____s are everything of value that is owned by a person or company. Any property or object of value that one possesses, usually considered as applicable to the payment of one's debts is considered an _____. Simplistically stated, _____s are things of value that can be readily converted into cash.

   a. AAAl
   b. A4e
   c. A Stake in the Outcome
   d. Asset

2. In accounting, a _____ is an asset on the balance sheet which is expected to be sold or otherwise used up in the near future, usually within one year, or one business cycle - whichever is longer. Typical _____s include cash, cash equivalents, accounts receivable, inventory, the portion of prepaid accounts which will be used within a year, and short-term investments.

   On the balance sheet, assets will typically be classified into _____s and long-term assets.

   a. Current asset
   b. Net income
   c. Matching principle
   d. Treasury stock

3. In finance, _____ are considered liabilities of the business that are to be settled in cash within the fiscal year or the operating cycle, whichever period is longer.

   For example accounts payable for goods, services or supplies that were purchased for use in the operation of the business and payable within a normal period of time would be _____.

   Bonds, mortgages and loans that are payable over a term exceeding one year would be fixed liabilities.

   a. Depreciation
   b. Current liabilities
   c. Generally accepted accounting principles
   d. Matching principle

4. _____ is a financial metric which represents operating liquidity available to a business. Along with fixed assets such as plant and equipment, _____ is considered a part of operating capital. It is calculated as current assets minus current liabilities.

   a. 28-hour day
   b. 1990 Clean Air Act
   c. 33 Strategies of War
   d. Working capital

5. _____ refers to the methods of practicing and using another person's business philosophy. The franchisor grants the independent operator the right to distribute its products, techniques, and trademarks for a percentage of gross monthly sales and a royalty fee. Various tangibles and intangibles such as national or international advertising, training, and other support services are commonly made available by the franchisor.

   a. 1990 Clean Air Act
   b. 28-hour day
   c. ServiceMaster
   d. Franchising

6. _____ is the capital that a business raises by taking out a loan. It is a loan made to a company that is normally repaid at some future date. _____ differs from equity or share capital because subscribers to _____ do not become part owners of the business, but are merely creditors, and the suppliers of _____ usually receive a contractually fixed annual percentage return on their loan, and this is known as the coupon rate.

   a. Novated lease
   b. Market value added
   c. Net worth
   d. Debt capital

Chapter 12. Sources of Financing: Debt and Equity

7. _____ is a type of private equity investment, most often a minority investment, in relatively mature companies that are looking for capital to expand or restructure operations, enter new markets or finance a significant acquisition without a change of control of the business.

Companies that seek _____, will often do so in order to finance a transformational event in their lifecycle. These companies are likely to be more mature than venture capital funded companies, able to generate revenue and operating profits but unable to generate sufficient cash to fund major expansions, acquisitions or other investments.

a. Growth capital
c. Seed round

b. Pension fund
d. Management buyout

8. In decision theory and estimation theory, the _____ of an estimator, $\hat{\theta}$, of an unknown parameter of the distribution, θ, is the expected value of the loss function

$$R(\theta, \hat{\theta}) = \mathbb{E}_\theta L(\theta, \hat{\theta}) = \int L(\theta, \hat{\theta})\, dP_\theta.$$

where dP_θ is a probability measure parametrized by θ.

- For a scalar parameter θ and a quadratic loss function,

$$L(\theta, \hat{\theta}) = (\theta - \hat{\theta})^2$$

the _____ function becomes the mean squared error of the estimate,

$$R(\theta, \hat{\theta}) = E_\theta (\theta - \hat{\theta})^2$$

- In density estimation, the unknown parameter is probability density itself. The loss function is typically chosen to be a norm in an appropriate function space. For example, for L^2 norm,

$$L(f, \hat{f}) = \|f - \hat{f}\|_2^2$$

the _____ function becomes the mean integrated squared error

$$R(f, \hat{f}) = E\|f - \hat{f}\|^2$$

a. Linear model
c. Financial modeling

b. Risk aversion
d. Risk

9. _____ is a civil designation for persons who are incorporated in a fixed or permanent way to a society or group: regular member of the working staff, permanent staff distinguished from a supernumerary.

The term '_____' and its counterpart, 'supernumerary,' originated in Spanish and Latin American academy and government; it is now also used in countries all over the world, such as France, the U.S., England, Italy, etc.

There are _____ members of surgical organizations, of universities, of gastronomical associations, etc.

   a. Affiliation
   b. Abraham Harold Maslow
   c. Numerary
   d. Adam Smith

10. An _____ is a person who has possession of an enterprise and assumes significant accountability for the inherent risks and the outcome. It is an ambitious leader who combines land, labor, and capital to create and market new goods or services. The term is a loanword from French and was first defined by the Irish economist Richard Cantillon.
   a. AAAI
   b. A4e
   c. A Stake in the Outcome
   d. Entrepreneur

11. _____ is a type of private equity capital typically provided to early-stage, high-potential, growth companies in the interest of generating a return through an eventual realization event such as an IPO or trade sale of the company. _____ investments are generally made as cash in exchange for shares in the invested company. It is typical for _____ investors to identify and back companies in high technology industries such as biotechnology and ICT.
   a. Limited liability corporation
   b. Seed round
   c. Private equity
   d. Venture capital

12. A _____ is a relatively new executive level position at a corporation, company, organization typically reporting directly to the CEO or board of directors. The _____ is responsible for a brand's image, experience, and promise, and propagating it throughout all aspects of the company. The brand officer oversees marketing, advertising, design, public relations and customer service departments.
   a. Chief executive officer
   b. Purchasing manager
   c. Director of communications
   d. Chief brand officer

13. _____ is one of the managerial functions like planning, organizing, staffing and directing. It is an important function because it helps to check the errors and to take the corrective action so that deviation from standards are minimized and stated goals of the organization are achieved in desired manner. According to modern concepts, _____ is a foreseeing action whereas earlier concept of _____ was used only when errors were detected. _____ in management means setting standards, measuring actual performance and taking corrective action.
   a. Schedule of reinforcement
   b. Control
   c. Turnover
   d. Decision tree pruning

14. _____ is the state or fact of exclusive rights and control over property, which may be an object, land/real estate or intellectual property. An _____ right is also referred to as title. The concept of _____ has existed for thousands of years and in all cultures.
   a. A4e
   b. A Stake in the Outcome
   c. Emanation of the state
   d. Ownership

Chapter 12. Sources of Financing: Debt and Equity

15. A _____ is a person or investment firm that makes venture investments, and these _____s are expected to bring managerial and technical expertise as well as capital to their investments. A venture capital fund refers to a pooled investment vehicle that primarily invests the financial capital of third-party investors in enterprises that are too risky for the standard capital markets or bank loans.

Venture capital is also associated with job creation, the knowledge economy and used as a proxy measure of innovation within an economic sector or geography.

a. Limited liability corporation
b. Limited partners
c. Private equity
d. Venture capitalist

16. _____ , also referred to simply as a 'public offering' or 'flotation,' is when a company issues common stock or shares to the public for the first time. They are often issued by smaller, younger companies seeking capital to expand, but can also be done by large privately-owned companies looking to become publicly traded.

In an _____ the issuer may obtain the assistance of an underwriting firm, which helps it determine what type of security to issue (common or preferred), best offering price and time to bring it to market.

a. Initial public offering
b. Outsourcing
c. Occupational Safety and Health Administration
d. Unemployment insurance

17. A _____ refers to how a corporation is perceived. It is a generally accepted image of what a company 'stands for'. The creation of a _____ is an exercise in perception management.

a. Marketing
b. Market development
c. Context analysis
d. Corporate image

18. The phrase mergers and _____s refers to the aspect of corporate strategy, corporate finance and management dealing with the buying, selling and combining of different companies that can aid, finance, or help a growing company in a given industry grow rapidly without having to create another business entity.

An _____, also known as a takeover or a buyout, is the buying of one company (the 'target') by another. An _____ may be friendly or hostile.

a. A4e
b. AAAI
c. A Stake in the Outcome
d. Acquisition

19. _____ is a concept in ethics with several meanings. It is often used synonymously with such concepts as responsibility, answerability, enforcement, blameworthiness, liability and other terms associated with the expectation of account-giving. As an aspect of governance, it has been central to discussions related to problems in both the public and private (corporation) worlds.

a. Usury
b. A Stake in the Outcome
c. Accountability
d. A4e

20. A mutual _____ or stockholder is an individual or company (including a corporation) that legally owns one or more shares of stock in a joint stock company. A company's _____s collectively own that company. Thus, the typical goal of such companies is to enhance _____ value.

Chapter 12. Sources of Financing: Debt and Equity

a. 1990 Clean Air Act
b. Stockholder
c. Free riding
d. Shareholder

21. _____ is a document outlining an agreement between two or more parties before the agreement is finalized. The concept is similar to the so-called heads of agreement. Such agreements may be Asset Purchase Agreements, Share Purchase Agreements, Joint-Venture Agreements and overall all Agreements which aim at closing a financially large deal.
   a. 33 Strategies of War
   b. 1990 Clean Air Act
   c. 28-hour day
   d. Letter of intent

22. Under the Securities Act of 1933, any offer to sell securities must either be registered with the SEC or meet an exemption. _____ contains three rules providing exemptions from the registration requirements, allowing some companies to offer and sell their securities without having to register the securities with the SEC. Rule 501 of Reg D contains definitions that apply to the rest of Reg D. Rule 502 contains the general conditions that must be met to take advantage of the exemptions under _____. Generally speaking, these conditions are (1) that all sales within a certain time period that are part of the same Reg D offering must be 'integrated', meaning they must be treated as one offering, (2) information and disclosures must be provided, (3) there must be no 'general solicitation', and (4) that the securities being sold contain restrictions on their resale.
   a. 1990 Clean Air Act
   b. Regulation D
   c. 33 Strategies of War
   d. 28-hour day

23. _____-model (SCOR(r)) is a process reference model developed by the management consulting firm PRTM and AMR Research and endorsed by the Supply-Chain Council (SCC) as the cross-industry de facto standard diagnostic tool for supply chain management. SCOR enables users to address, improve, and communicate supply chain management practices within and between all interested parties in the Extended Enterprise.

   SCOR(r) is a management tool, spanning from the supplier's supplier to the customer's customer. The model has been developed by the members of the Council on a volunteer basis to describe the business activities associated with all phases of satisfying a customer's demand.

   a. Delayed differentiation
   b. Supply-Chain Operations Reference
   c. Supply chain management software
   d. Supply Chain Risk Management

24. A _____ is a funding round of securities which are sold without a initial public offering, usually to a small number of chosen private investors. In the United States, these placements are not subject to the Securities Act of 1933 and do not have to be registered with the Securities and Exchange Commission, although the sale must conform to SEC rules. _____s may typically consist of stocks, shares or warrants and purchasers are often institutional investors such as banks, insurance companies or pension funds.
   a. Choquet integral
   b. Niche market
   c. Labor intensive
   d. Private Placement

25. _____ is a term applied in many countries to a reference interest rate used by banks. The term originally indicated the rate of interest at which banks lent to favored customers, i.e., those with high credibility, though this is no longer always the case. Some variable interest rates may be expressed as a percentage above or below _____.
   a. Reserve requirement
   b. Lock box
   c. 1990 Clean Air Act
   d. Prime rate

26. A _____ is a business that is privately owned and operated, with a small number of employees and relatively low volume of sales. The legal definition of 'small' often varies by country and industry, but is generally under 100 employees in the United States and under 50 employees in the European Union. In comparison, the definition of mid-sized business by the number of employees is generally under 500 in the U.S. and 250 for the European Union.
   a. Pre-determined overhead rate
   b. Golden Boot Compensation
   c. Critical Success Factor
   d. Small Business

27. The _____ is a United States government agency that provides support to small businesses.

The mission of the _____ is 'to maintain and strengthen the nation's economy by enabling the establishment and viability of small businesses and by assisting in the economic recovery of communities after disasters.'

The _____ makes loans directly to businesses and acts as a guarantor on bank loans. In some circumstances it also makes loans to victims of natural disasters, works to get government procurement contracts for small businesses, and assists businesses with management, technical and training issues.

   a. 1990 Clean Air Act
   b. Small Business Administration
   c. 28-hour day
   d. 33 Strategies of War

28. A _____ is any credit source extended to a business by a bank or financial institution. A _____ may take several forms such as cash credit, overdraft, demand loan, export packing credit, term loan, discounting or purchase of commercial bills etc. It is like an account that can readily be tapped into if the need arises or not touched at all and saved for emergencies.
   a. 1990 Clean Air Act
   b. 28-hour day
   c. 33 Strategies of War
   d. Line of credit

29. Title _____s serve as guarantees to the recipient of property, ensuring that the recipient receives what he or she bargained for. The English _____s of title, sometimes included in deeds to real property, are that the grantor is lawfully seized (in fee simple) of the property, (2) that the grantor has the right to convey the property to the grantee, (3) that the property is conveyed without encumbrances (this _____ is frequently modified to allow for certain encumbrances), (4) that the grantor has done no act to encumber the property, (5) that the grantee shall have quiet possession of the property, and (6) that the grantor will execute such further assurances of the land as may be requisite (Nos. 3 and 4, which overlap significantly, are sometimes treated as one item.)
   a. Hostile work environment
   b. Trade secret
   c. Business valuation
   d. Covenant

30. _____ is one of a series of accounting transactions dealing with the billing of customers who owe money to a person, company or organization for goods and services that have been provided to the customer. In most business entities this is typically done by generating an invoice and mailing or electronically delivering it to the customer, who in turn must pay it within an established timeframe called credit or payment terms.

An example of a common payment term is Net 30, meaning payment is due in the amount of the invoice 30 days from the date of invoice.

Chapter 12. Sources of Financing: Debt and Equity

a. Other revenue
c. Accumulated Depreciation
b. A Stake in the Outcome
d. Accounts receivable

31. _____ is a form of short-term borrowing often used to improve a company's working capital and cash flow position.

_____ allows a business to draw money against its sales invoices before the customer has actually paid. To do this, the business borrows a percentage of the value of its sales ledger from a finance company, effectively using the unpaid sales invoices as collateral for the borrowing.

a. A Stake in the Outcome
c. A4e
b. AAAI
d. Invoice discounting

32. _____ exists when one firm provides goods or services to a customer with an agreement to bill them later, or receive a shipment or service from a supplier under an agreement to pay them later. It can be viewed as an essential element of capitalization in an operating business because it can reduce the required capital investment to operate the business if it is managed properly. _____ is the largest use of capital for a majority of business to business (B2B) sellers in the United States and is a critical source of capital for a majority of all businesses.

a. Countertrade
c. Trade credit
b. Buy-sell agreement
d. 1990 Clean Air Act

33. A _____ is typically described as a deliberate plan of action to guide decisions and achieve rational outcome(s.) However, the term may also be used to denote what is actually done, even though it is unplanned.

The term may apply to government, private sector organizations and groups, and individuals.

a. 28-hour day
c. 33 Strategies of War
b. 1990 Clean Air Act
d. Policy

34. _____ is an advertisement in which a particular product specifically mentions a competitor by name for the express purpose of showing why the competitor is inferior to the product naming it.

This should not be confused with parody advertisements, where a fictional product is being advertised for the purpose of poking fun at the particular advertisement, nor should it be confused with the use of a coined brand name for the purpose of comparing the product without actually naming an actual competitor. ('Wikipedia tastes better and is less filling than the Encyclopedia Galactica.')

In the 1980s, during what has been referred to as the cola wars, soft-drink manufacturer Pepsi ran a series of advertisements where people, caught on hidden camera, in a blind taste test, chose Pepsi over rival Coca-Cola.

a. 33 Strategies of War
c. 1990 Clean Air Act
b. 28-hour day
d. Comparative advertising

35. _____ is the process of sharing of skills, knowledge, technologies, methods of manufacturing, samples of manufacturing and facilities among governments and other institutions to ensure that scientific and technological developments are accessible to a wider range of users who can then further develop and exploit the technology into new products, processes, applications, materials or services. It is closely related to (and may arguably be considered a subset of) Knowledge transfer. Related terms, used almost synonymously, include 'technology valorisation' and 'technology commercialisation'.

   a. Munn v. Illinois
   b. Competition law
   c. Mediation
   d. Technology Transfer

36. _____ is exchange of capital, goods, and services across international borders or territories. In most countries, it represents a significant share of gross domestic product (GDP.) While _____ has been present throughout much of history, its economic, social, and political importance has been on the rise in recent centuries.

   a. AAAI
   b. A4e
   c. A Stake in the Outcome
   d. International Trade

Chapter 13. Choosing the Right Location and Layout

1. _____ or _____ data refers to selected population characteristics as used in government, marketing or opinion research, or the _____ profiles used in such research. Note the distinction from the term 'demography' Commonly-used _____s include race, age, income, disabilities, mobility (in terms of travel time to work or number of vehicles available), educational attainment, home ownership, employment status, and even location.
    a. Affiliation
    b. Abraham Harold Maslow
    c. Adam Smith
    d. Demographic

2. _____ is an integrated communications-based process through which individuals and communities discover that existing and newly-identified needs and wants may be satisfied by the products and services of others.

    _____ is defined by the American _____ Association as the activity, set of institutions, and processes for creating, communicating, delivering, and exchanging offerings that have value for customers, clients, partners, and society at large. The term developed from the original meaning which referred literally to going to market, as in shopping, or going to a market to buy or sell goods or services.

    a. Disruptive technology
    b. Market development
    c. Customer relationship management
    d. Marketing

3. _____ refers to the movement of cash into or out of a business or financial product. It is usually measured during a specified, finite period of time. Measurement of _____ can be used

    - to determine a project's rate of return or value. The time of _____s into and out of projects are used as inputs in financial models such as internal rate of return, and net present value.
    - to determine problems with a business's liquidity. Being profitable does not necessarily mean being liquid. A company can fail because of a shortage of cash, even while profitable.
    - as an alternate measure of a business's profits when it is believed that accrual accounting concepts do not represent economic realities. For example, a company may be notionally profitable but generating little operational cash (as may be the case for a company that barters its products rather than selling for cash.) In such a case, the company may be deriving additional operating cash by issuing shares evaluating default risk, re-investment requirements, etc.

    _____ is a generic term used differently depending on the context. It may be defined by users for their own purposes.

    a. Cash flow
    b. Sweat equity
    c. Gross profit
    d. Gross profit margin

4. _____ is a financial metric which represents operating liquidity available to a business. Along with fixed assets such as plant and equipment, _____ is considered a part of operating capital. It is calculated as current assets minus current liabilities.
    a. 28-hour day
    b. 1990 Clean Air Act
    c. 33 Strategies of War
    d. Working Capital

5. A _____ is a compensation, usually financial, received by a worker in exchange for their labor.

Compensation in terms of _____s is given to worker and compensation in terms of salary is given to employees. Compensation is a monetary benefits given to employees in returns of the services provided by them.

Chapter 13. Choosing the Right Location and Layout

a. Performance-related pay
c. Wage
b. State Compensation Insurance Fund
d. Profit-sharing agreement

6. In mainstream economic theories, the supply of labor is the number of total hours that workers wish to work at a given real wage rate. Realisticly, the _____ is a fuction of various factors within an economy. For instance, overpopulation increases the number of available workers driving down wages and can result in high unemployment.
   a. 33 Strategies of War
   c. 1990 Clean Air Act
   b. Labor supply
   d. 28-hour day

7. The term '_____' refers to the concept of collecting information and attempting to spot a pattern in the information. In some fields of study, the term '_____' has more formally-defined meanings.

In project management _____ is a mathematical technique that uses historical results to predict future outcome.

   a. Trend analysis
   c. Least squares
   b. Stepwise regression
   d. Regression analysis

8. A _____ is a type of business entity in which partners (owners) share with each other the profits or losses of the business. _____s are often favored over corporations for taxation purposes, as the _____ structure does not generally incur a tax on profits before it is distributed to the partners (i.e. there is no dividend tax levied.) However, depending on the _____ structure and the jurisdiction in which it operates, owners of a _____ may be exposed to greater personal liability than they would as shareholders of a corporation.
   a. Mediation
   c. Partnership
   b. Due process
   d. Federal Employers Liability Act

9. In economics, business, retail, and accounting, a _____ is the value of money that has been used up to produce something, and hence is not available for use anymore. In economics, a _____ is an alternative that is given up as a result of a decision. In business, the _____ may be one of acquisition, in which case the amount of money expended to acquire it is counted as _____.
   a. Fixed costs
   c. Cost allocation
   b. Cost overrun
   d. Cost

10. _____ is an advertisement in which a particular product specifically mentions a competitor by name for the express purpose of showing why the competitor is inferior to the product naming it.

This should not be confused with parody advertisements, where a fictional product is being advertised for the purpose of poking fun at the particular advertisement, nor should it be confused with the use of a coined brand name for the purpose of comparing the product without actually naming an actual competitor. ('Wikipedia tastes better and is less filling than the Encyclopedia Galactica.')

In the 1980s, during what has been referred to as the cola wars, soft-drink manufacturer Pepsi ran a series of advertisements where people, caught on hidden camera, in a blind taste test, chose Pepsi over rival Coca-Cola.

a. 33 Strategies of War
b. 1990 Clean Air Act
c. Comparative advertising
d. 28-hour day

11. _____, commonly known as e-commerce, consists of the buying and selling of products or services over electronic systems such as the Internet and other computer networks. The amount of trade conducted electronically has grown extraordinarily with widespread Internet usage. The use of commerce is conducted in this way, spurring and drawing on innovations in electronic funds transfer, supply chain management, Internet marketing, online transaction processing, electronic data interchange (EDI), inventory management systems, and automated data collection systems.
   a. Electronic Commerce
   b. Online shopping
   c. A4e
   d. A Stake in the Outcome

12. In finance, an _____ is a contract between a buyer and a seller that gives the buyer the right--but not the obligation--to buy or to sell a particular asset (the underlying asset) at a later day at an agreed price. In return for granting the _____, the seller collects a payment (the premium) from the buyer. A call _____ gives the buyer the right to buy the underlying asset; a put _____ gives the buyer of the _____ the right to sell the underlying asset.
   a. A4e
   b. Option
   c. A Stake in the Outcome
   d. AAAI

13. _____ are programs designed to accelerate the successful development of entrepreneurial companies through an array of business support resources and services, developed and orchestrated by incubator management and offered both in the incubator and through its network of contacts. Incubators vary in the way they deliver their services, in their organizational structure, and in the types of clients they serve. Successful completion of a business incubation program increases the likelihood that a start-up company will stay in business for the long term: Historically, 87% of incubator graduates stay in business.
   a. 1990 Clean Air Act
   b. 33 Strategies of War
   c. Business incubators
   d. 28-hour day

14. _____ refers to increasing the spiritual, political, social or economic strength of individuals and communities. It often involves the empowered developing confidence in their own capacities.

The term Human _____ covers a vast landscape of meanings, interpretations, definitions and disciplines ranging from psychology and philosophy to the highly commercialized Self-Help industry and Motivational sciences.

   a. A Stake in the Outcome
   b. Empowerment
   c. AAAI
   d. A4e

15. The _____ of 1990 (ADA) is the short title of United States (Pub.L. 101-336, 104 Stat. 327, enacted July 26, 1990), codified at 42 U.S.C. § 12101 et seq. It was signed into law on July 26, 1990, by President George H. W. Bush, and later amended with changes effective January 1, 2009. The ADA is a wide-ranging civil rights law that prohibits, under certain circumstances, discrimination based on disability. It affords similar protections against discrimination to Americans with disabilities as the Civil Rights Act of 1964,
   a. Americans with Disabilities Act
   b. Equal Pay Act of 1963
   c. Australian labour law
   d. Employment discrimination

16. _____ is a medical condition in which the median nerve is compressed at the wrist, leading to paresthesias, numbness and muscle weakness in the hand. The diagnosis of _____ is often misapplied to patients who have activity-related arm pain.

Most cases of _____ are idiopathic (without known cause); genetic factors determine most of the risk, and the role of arm use and other environmental factors is disputed.

   a. Carpal tunnel syndrome
   c. 28-hour day
   b. 33 Strategies of War
   d. 1990 Clean Air Act

17. _____s is the science of designing the job, equipment, and workplace to fit the worker. Proper _____ design is necessary to prevent repetitive strain injuries, which can develop over time and can lead to long-term disability.

_____s is concerned with the 'fit' between people and their work.

   a. AAAI
   c. A Stake in the Outcome
   b. A4e
   d. Ergonomic

18. _____ generally refers to a list of all planned expenses and revenues. It is a plan for saving and spending. A _____ is an important concept in microeconomics, which uses a _____ line to illustrate the trade-offs between two or more goods.
   a. Budget
   c. 33 Strategies of War
   b. 1990 Clean Air Act
   d. 28-hour day

Chapter 14. Global Aspects of Entrepreneurship

1. An _____ is a person who has possession of an enterprise and assumes significant accountability for the inherent risks and the outcome. It is an ambitious leader who combines land, labor, and capital to create and market new goods or services. The term is a loanword from French and was first defined by the Irish economist Richard Cantillon.
   a. A Stake in the Outcome
   b. AAAI
   c. A4e
   d. Entrepreneur

2. _____ according to Onuoha (2007) is the practice of starting new organizations or revitalizing mature organizations, particularly new businesses generally in response to identified opportunities. _____ is often a difficult undertaking, as a vast majority of new businesses fail. Entrepreneurial activities are substantially different depending on the type of organization that is being started.
   a. A4e
   b. A Stake in the Outcome
   c. AAAI
   d. Entrepreneurship

3. A _____ is a business that is privately owned and operated, with a small number of employees and relatively low volume of sales. The legal definition of 'small' often varies by country and industry, but is generally under 100 employees in the United States and under 50 employees in the European Union. In comparison, the definition of mid-sized business by the number of employees is generally under 500 in the U.S. and 250 for the European Union.
   a. Golden Boot Compensation
   b. Pre-determined overhead rate
   c. Critical Success Factor
   d. Small business

4. _____ refers to the movement of cash into or out of a business or financial product. It is usually measured during a specified, finite period of time. Measurement of _____ can be used

   - to determine a project's rate of return or value. The time of _____s into and out of projects are used as inputs in financial models such as internal rate of return, and net present value.
   - to determine problems with a business's liquidity. Being profitable does not necessarily mean being liquid. A company can fail because of a shortage of cash, even while profitable.
   - as an alternate measure of a business's profits when it is believed that accrual accounting concepts do not represent economic realities. For example, a company may be notionally profitable but generating little operational cash (as may be the case for a company that barters its products rather than selling for cash.) In such a case, the company may be deriving additional operating cash by issuing shares evaluating default risk, re-investment requirements, etc.

   _____ is a generic term used differently depending on the context. It may be defined by users for their own purposes.

   a. Sweat equity
   b. Gross profit
   c. Gross profit margin
   d. Cash flow

5. _____ is the branch of economics that studies the dynamics of exchange rates, foreign investment, and how these affect international trade. It also studies international projects, international investments and capital flows, and trade deficits. It includes the study of futures, options and currency swaps.
   a. AAAI
   b. A Stake in the Outcome
   c. A4e
   d. International finance

Chapter 14. Global Aspects of Entrepreneurship

6. The _____ or gross domestic income (GDI), a basic measure of an economy's economic performance, is the market value of all final goods and services made within the borders of a nation in a year. _____ can be defined in three ways, all of which are conceptually identical. First, it is equal to the total expenditures for all final goods and services produced within the country in a stipulated period of time (usually a 365-day year).
   a. Productivity management
   b. Perfect competition
   c. Human capital
   d. Gross domestic product

7. _____ is exchange of capital, goods, and services across international borders or territories. In most countries, it represents a significant share of gross domestic product (GDP.) While _____ has been present throughout much of history , its economic, social, and political importance has been on the rise in recent centuries.
   a. International Trade
   b. A Stake in the Outcome
   c. A4e
   d. AAAI

8. An _____ is an organization founded and funded by businesses that operate in a specific industry. An industry trade association participates in public relations activities such as advertising, education, political donations, lobbying and publishing, but its main focus is collaboration between companies, or standardization. Associations may offer other services, such as producing conferences, networking or charitable events or offering classes or educational materials.
   a. AAAI
   b. A Stake in the Outcome
   c. A4e
   d. Industry trade group

9. _____ exists when one firm provides goods or services to a customer with an agreement to bill them later, or receive a shipment or service from a supplier under an agreement to pay them later. It can be viewed as an essential element of capitalization in an operating business because it can reduce the required capital investment to operate the business if it is managed properly. _____ is the largest use of capital for a majority of business to business (B2B) sellers in the United States and is a critical source of capital for a majority of all businesses.
   a. Buy-sell agreement
   b. Countertrade
   c. 1990 Clean Air Act
   d. Trade credit

10. The _____ is the Cabinet department of the United States government concerned with promoting economic growth. It was originally created as the _____ and Labor on February 14, 1903. It was subsequently renamed to the Department of Commerce on March 4, 1913, and its bureaus and agencies specializing in labor were transferred to the new Department of Labor.
    a. A Stake in the Outcome
    b. AAAI
    c. United States Department of Commerce
    d. A4e

11. A _____ is an entity formed between two or more parties to undertake economic activity together. The parties agree to create a new entity by both contributing equity, and they then share in the revenues, expenses, and control of the enterprise. The venture can be for one specific project only, or a continuing business relationship such as the Fuji Xerox _____.
    a. Civil Rights Act of 1991
    b. Meritor Savings Bank v. Vinson
    c. Patent
    d. Joint venture

12. _____ is an advertisement in which a particular product specifically mentions a competitor by name for the express purpose of showing why the competitor is inferior to the product naming it.

This should not be confused with parody advertisements, where a fictional product is being advertised for the purpose of poking fun at the particular advertisement, nor should it be confused with the use of a coined brand name for the purpose of comparing the product without actually naming an actual competitor. ('Wikipedia tastes better and is less filling than the Encyclopedia Galactica.')

In the 1980s, during what has been referred to as the cola wars, soft-drink manufacturer Pepsi ran a series of advertisements where people, caught on hidden camera, in a blind taste test, chose Pepsi over rival Coca-Cola.

a. 28-hour day
b. 33 Strategies of War
c. 1990 Clean Air Act
d. Comparative advertising

13. _____ refers to the methods of practicing and using another person's business philosophy. The franchisor grants the independent operator the right to distribute its products, techniques, and trademarks for a percentage of gross monthly sales and a royalty fee. Various tangibles and intangibles such as national or international advertising, training, and other support services are commonly made available by the franchisor.

a. Franchising
b. 28-hour day
c. ServiceMaster
d. 1990 Clean Air Act

14. Marketing research is a form of business research and is generally divided into two categories: consumer _____ and business-to-business (B2B) _____, which was previously known as industrial marketing research. Consumer marketing research studies the buying habits of individual people while business-to-business marketing research investigates the markets for products sold by one business to another.

Consumer _____ is a form of applied sociology that concentrates on understanding the behaviours, whims and preferences, of consumers in a market-based economy, and aims to understand the effects and comparative success of marketing campaigns.

a. Questionnaire
b. Market research
c. Mystery shoppers
d. Questionnaire construction

15. _____ is a financial metric which represents operating liquidity available to a business. Along with fixed assets such as plant and equipment, _____ is considered a part of operating capital. It is calculated as current assets minus current liabilities.

a. 33 Strategies of War
b. Working Capital
c. 1990 Clean Air Act
d. 28-hour day

16. A standard, commercial _____ is a document issued mostly by a financial institution, used primarily in trade finance, which usually provides an irrevocable payment undertaking.

The LC can also be the source of payment for a traction, meaning that redeeming the _____ will pay an exporter. Letters of credit are used primarily in international trade transactions of significant value, for deals between a supplier in one country and a customer in another.

a. False Claims Act
b. Sarbanes-Oxley Act of 2002
c. Diminishing returns
d. Letter of credit

17. _____ generally refers to a list of all planned expenses and revenues. It is a plan for saving and spending. A _____ is an important concept in microeconomics, which uses a _____ line to illustrate the trade-offs between two or more goods.

a. 1990 Clean Air Act
b. 28-hour day
c. 33 Strategies of War
d. Budget

18. The _____ is an international organization designed by its founders to supervise and liberalize international trade. The organization officially commenced on 1 January 1995, under the Marrakesh Agreement, succeeding the 1947 General Agreement on Tariffs and Trade (GATT.)

The _____ deals with regulation of trade between participating countries; it provides a framework for negotiating and formalising trade agreements, and a dispute resolution process aimed at enforcing participants' adherence to _____ agreements which are signed by representatives of member governments and ratified by their parliaments.

a. Network planning and design
b. 1990 Clean Air Act
c. National Institute for Occupational Safety and Health
d. World Trade Organization

19. A _____ is a general term that describes any government policy or regulation that restricts international trade. The barriers can take many forms, including the following terms that include many restrictions in international trade within multiple countries that import and export any items of trade.

- Import duty
- Import licenses
- Export licenses
- Import quotas
- Tariffs
- Subsidies
- Non-tariff barriers to trade
- Voluntary Export Restraints
- Local Content Requirements
- Embargo

Most _____s work on the same principle: the imposition of some sort of cost on trade that raises the price of the traded products. If two or more nations repeatedly use _____s against each other, then a trade war results.

a. Customs brokerage
b. Most favoured nation
c. Trade barrier
d. Trade creation

20. _____ is a type of trade policy that allows traders to act and transact without interference from government. Thus, the policy permits trading partners mutual gains from trade, with goods and services produced according to the theory of comparative advantage.

Under a _____ policy, prices are a reflection of true supply and demand, and are the sole determinant of resource allocation.

- a. 28-hour day
- b. 33 Strategies of War
- c. 1990 Clean Air Act
- d. Free Trade

21. _____ is a designated group of countries that have agreed to eliminate tariffs, quotas and preferences on most (if not all) goods and services traded between them. It can be considered the second stage of economic integration. Countries choose this kind of economic integration form if their economical structures are complementary.
- a. 28-hour day
- b. 1990 Clean Air Act
- c. 33 Strategies of War
- d. Free trade area

22. The _____ is a treaty of the World Trade Organization (WTO) that entered into force in January 1995 as a result of the Uruguay Round negotiations. The treaty was created to extend the multilateral trading system to service sector, in the same way the General Agreement on Tariffs and Trade (GATT) provides such a system for merchandise trade.
- a. 33 Strategies of War
- b. 28-hour day
- c. 1990 Clean Air Act
- d. General Agreement on Trade in Services

23. The _____ is a trilateral trade bloc in North America created by the governments of the United States, Canada, and Mexico. The agreement creating the trade bloc came into force on January 1, 1994. It superseded the Canada-United States Free Trade Agreement between the U.S. and Canada.
- a. Trade union
- b. Career portfolios
- c. Business war game
- d. North American Free Trade Agreement

Chapter 15. Leading the Growing Company and Planning for Management Succession

1. _____ has been described as the 'process of social influence in which one person can enlist the aid and support of others in the accomplishment of a common task' . A definition more inclusive of followers comes from Alan Keith of Genentech who said '_____ is ultimately about creating a way for people to contribute to making something extraordinary happen.'

_____ is one of the most salient aspects of the organizational context. However, defining _____ has been challenging.

   a. Situational leadership
   b. 1990 Clean Air Act
   c. 28-hour day
   d. Leadership

2. A _____ is a business that is privately owned and operated, with a small number of employees and relatively low volume of sales. The legal definition of 'small' often varies by country and industry, but is generally under 100 employees in the United States and under 50 employees in the European Union. In comparison, the definition of mid-sized business by the number of employees is generally under 500 in the U.S. and 250 for the European Union.
   a. Critical Success Factor
   b. Golden Boot Compensation
   c. Pre-determined overhead rate
   d. Small business

3. The _____ was an evolution of developed countries from an industrial/manufacturing-based wealth producing economy into a service sector asset based economy, brought about by globalization and currency manipulation by governments and their central banks. Some analysts claimed that this change in the economic structure of the United States had created a state of permanent steady growth, low unemployment, and immunity to boom and bust macroeconomic cycles. They believed that the change rendered obsolete many business practices.
   a. New economy
   b. 33 Strategies of War
   c. 28-hour day
   d. 1990 Clean Air Act

4. _____ refers to the process of screening, and selecting qualified people for a job at an organization or firm mid- and large-size organizations and companies often retain professional recruiters or outsource some of the process to _____ agencies. External _____ is the process of attracting and selecting employees from outside the organization.

The _____ industry has four main types of agencies: employment agencies, _____ websites and job search engines, 'headhunters' for executive and professional _____, and in-house _____.

   a. Labour hire
   b. Referral recruitment
   c. Recruitment
   d. Recruitment Process Outsourcing

5. A _____ is typically described as a deliberate plan of action to guide decisions and achieve rational outcome(s.) However, the term may also be used to denote what is actually done, even though it is unplanned.

The term may apply to government, private sector organizations and groups, and individuals.

   a. 1990 Clean Air Act
   b. 33 Strategies of War
   c. Policy
   d. 28-hour day

Chapter 15. Leading the Growing Company and Planning for Management Succession 91

6. _____ is an internal recruitment method employed by organisations to identify potential candidates from their existing employees social networks. An _____ scheme encourages a company's existing employees to select and recruit the suitable candidates from their social networks. As a reward, the employer typically pays the referring employee a referral bonus.
   a. Employee referral
   b. Executive search
   c. Internet recruiting
   d. Employment agency

7. The _____, commonly known as the DOT was the creation of the U.S. Employment Service, which used its thousands of occupational definitions to match job seekers to jobs from 1939 to the late 1990s.

Before 1939, nationwide occupational information was not conveniently reported by the Employment Service. By 1939, it had become clear to the Employment service that a standardized volume of job definitions was needed for employment-related purposes.

   a. Dictionary of Occupational Titles
   b. 28-hour day
   c. 1990 Clean Air Act
   d. 33 Strategies of War

8. _____ refers to various methodologies for analyzing the requirements of a job.

The general purpose of _____ is to document the requirements of a job and the work performed. Job and task analysis is performed as a basis for later improvements, including: definition of a job domain; describing a job; developing performance appraisals, selection systems, promotion criteria, training needs assessment, and compensation plans.

   a. Work design
   b. Hersey-Blanchard situational theory
   c. Job analysis
   d. Management process

9. A _____ is a list of the general tasks and responsibilities of a position. Typically, it also includes to whom the position reports, specifications such as the qualifications needed by the person in the job, salary range for the position, etc. A _____ is usually developed by conducting a job analysis, which includes examining the tasks and sequences of tasks necessary to perform the job.
   a. Recruitment
   b. Job description
   c. Recruitment advertising
   d. Recruitment Process Insourcing

10. In mathematical logic, _____ is a valid argument and rule of inference which makes the inference that, if the conjunction A and B is true, then A is true, and B is true.

In formal language:

$$A \wedge B \vdash A$$

or

$$A \wedge B \vdash B$$

Chapter 15. Leading the Growing Company and Planning for Management Succession

The argument has one premise, namely a conjunction, and one often uses _____ in longer arguments to derive one of the conjuncts.

An example in English:

It's raining and it's pouring.

a. Fuzzy logic
c. 1990 Clean Air Act
b. Simplification
d. Validity

11. _____ is a contract between two parties, one being the employer and the other being the employee. An employee may be defined as: 'A person in the service of another under any contract of hire, express or implied, oral or written, where the employer has the power or right to control and direct the employee in the material details of how the work is to be performed.' Black's Law Dictionary page 471 (5th ed. 1979.)

a. Employment counsellor
c. Employment
b. Employment rate
d. Exit interview

12. The term _____ was created by President Lyndon B. Johnson when he signed Executive Order 11246 on September 24, 1965, created to prohibit federal contractors from discriminating against employees on the basis of race, sex, creed, religion, color, or national origin. In more recent times, most employers have also added sexual orientation to the list of non-discrimination.

The Executive Order also required contractors to implement affirmative action plans to increase the participation of minorities and women in the workplace.

a. AAAI
c. Equal Employment Opportunity
b. A4e
d. A Stake in the Outcome

13. The U.S. _____ is a federal agency whose goal is ending employment discrimination. The _____ investigates discrimination complaints based on an individual's race, color, national origin, religion, sex, age, disability and retaliation for reporting and/or opposing a discriminatory practice. The Commission is also tasked with filing suits on behalf of alleged victim(s) of discrimination against employers and as an adjudicatory for claims of discrimination brought against federal agencies.

a. Equal Employment Opportunity Commission
c. Airbus Industrie
b. ARCO
d. Airbus SAS

14. _____ is an idea in the field of Organizational studies and management which describes the psychology, attitudes, experiences, beliefs and Values (personal and cultural values) of an organization. It has been defined as 'the specific collection of values and norms that are shared by people and groups in an organization and that control the way they interact with each other and with stakeholders outside the organization.'

Chapter 15. Leading the Growing Company and Planning for Management Succession

This definition continues to explain organizational values also known as 'beliefs and ideas about what kinds of goals members of an organization should pursue and ideas about the appropriate kinds or standards of behavior organizational members should use to achieve these goals. From organizational values develop organizational norms, guidelines or expectations that prescribe appropriate kinds of behavior by employees in particular situations and control the behavior of organizational members towards one another.'

_____ is not the same as corporate culture.

a. Organizational effectiveness
c. Organizational development
b. Organizational culture
d. Union shop

15. _____ are employee benefit programs offered by many employers, typically in conjunction with a health insurance plan. _____s are intended to help employees deal with personal problems that might adversely impact their work performance, health, and well-being. _____s generally include assessment, short-term counseling and referral services for employees and their household members.

a. Employee benefits
c. A4e
b. Employee assistance programs
d. A Stake in the Outcome

16. The 'business case for _____', theorizes that in a global marketplace, a company that employs a diverse workforce (both men and women, people of many generations, people from ethnically and racially diverse backgrounds etc.) is better able to understand the demographics of the marketplace it serves and is thus better equipped to thrive in that marketplace than a company that has a more limited range of employee demographics.

An additional corollary suggests that a company that supports the _____ of its workforce can also improve employee satisfaction, productivity and retention.

a. Kanban
c. Trademark
b. Diversity
d. Virtual team

17. Various _____ can be employed dependent on the culture of the business, the nature of the task, the nature of the workforce and the personality and skills of the leaders. This idea was further developed by Robert Tannenbaum and Warren H. Schmidt (1958, 1973) who argued that the style of leadership is dependent upon the prevailing circumstance; therefore leaders should exercise a range of leadership styles and should deploy them as appropriate.

An Autocratic or authoritarian manager makes all the decisions, keeping the information and decision making among the senior management.

a. 33 Strategies of War
c. Management styles
b. 28-hour day
d. 1990 Clean Air Act

18. A _____ is a type of business entity in which partners (owners) share with each other the profits or losses of the business. _____s are often favored over corporations for taxation purposes, as the _____ structure does not generally incur a tax on profits before it is distributed to the partners (i.e. there is no dividend tax levied.) However, depending on the _____ structure and the jurisdiction in which it operates, owners of a _____ may be exposed to greater personal liability than they would as shareholders of a corporation.

a. Partnership
b. Due process
c. Mediation
d. Federal Employers Liability Act

19. An _____ is a person who has possession of an enterprise and assumes significant accountability for the inherent risks and the outcome. It is an ambitious leader who combines land, labor, and capital to create and market new goods or services. The term is a loanword from French and was first defined by the Irish economist Richard Cantillon.
a. A4e
b. A Stake in the Outcome
c. AAAI
d. Entrepreneur

20. _____ refers to increasing the spiritual, political, social or economic strength of individuals and communities. It often involves the empowered developing confidence in their own capacities.

The term Human _____ covers a vast landscape of meanings, interpretations, definitions and disciplines ranging from psychology and philosophy to the highly commercialized Self-Help industry and Motivational sciences.

a. AAAI
b. A Stake in the Outcome
c. Empowerment
d. A4e

21. _____ is a management technique pioneered by Michael Phillips in San Francisco in the late '60's and early '70s. The concept's most visible success was by Jack Stack and his team at SRC Holdings and popularized in 1995 by John Case. The technique is to give employees all relevant financial information about the company so they can make better decisions as workers.
a. AAAI
b. A4e
c. A Stake in the Outcome
d. Open-book management

22. In organizational development (OD), _____ is the application of Socio-Technical Systems principles and techniques to the humanization of work.

The aims of _____ to improved job satisfaction, to improved through-put, to improved quality and to reduced employee problems, e.g., grievances, absenteeism.

Under scientific management people would be directed by reason and the problems of industrial unrest would be appropriately (i.e., scientifically) addressed.

a. Work design
b. Path-goal theory
c. Management process
d. Graduate recruitment

23. _____ means increasing the scope of a job through extending the range of its job duties and responsibilities. This contradicts the principles of specialisation and the division of labour whereby work is divided into small units, each of which is performed repetitively by an individual worker. Some motivational theories suggest that the boredom and alienation caused by the division of labour can actually cause efficiency to fall.
a. Delayering
b. Job enlargement
c. Centralization
d. Mock interview

Chapter 15. Leading the Growing Company and Planning for Management Succession

24. _____ is an attempt to motivate employees by giving them the opportunity to use the range of their abilities. It is an idea that was developed by the American psychologist Frederick Herzberg in the 1950s. It can be contrasted to job enlargement which simply increases the number of tasks without changing the challenge.
   a. C-A-K-E
   b. Cash cow
   c. Catfish effect
   d. Job enrichment

25. _____ is an approach to management development where an individual is moved through a schedule of assignments designed to give him or her a breadth of exposure to the entire operation.

   _____ is also practiced to allow qualified employees to gain more insights into the processes of a company, and to reduce boredom and increase job satisfaction through job variation.

   The term _____ can also mean the scheduled exchange of persons in offices, especially in public offices, prior to the end of incumbency or the legislative period.

   a. 1990 Clean Air Act
   b. 33 Strategies of War
   c. 28-hour day
   d. Job rotation

26. _____, commonly known as e-commerce, consists of the buying and selling of products or services over electronic systems such as the Internet and other computer networks. The amount of trade conducted electronically has grown extraordinarily with widespread Internet usage. The use of commerce is conducted in this way, spurring and drawing on innovations in electronic funds transfer, supply chain management, Internet marketing, online transaction processing, electronic data interchange (EDI), inventory management systems, and automated data collection systems.
   a. Online shopping
   b. A Stake in the Outcome
   c. A4e
   d. Electronic Commerce

27. _____ describes the situation when output from (or information about the result of) an event or phenomenon in the past will influence the same event/phenomenon in the present or future. When an event is part of a chain of cause-and-effect that forms a circuit or loop, then the event is said to 'feed back' into itself.

   _____ is also a synonym for:

   - _____ signal; the information about the initial event that is the basis for subsequent modification of the event.
   - _____ loop; the causal path that leads from the initial generation of the _____ signal to the subsequent modification of the event.

   _____ is a mechanism, process or signal that is looped back to control a system within itself. Such a loop is called a _____ loop.

   a. Feedback loop
   b. Feedback
   c. Positive feedback
   d. 1990 Clean Air Act

Chapter 15. Leading the Growing Company and Planning for Management Succession

28. _____ is a variable work schedule, in contrast to traditional work arrangements requiring employees to work a standard 9am to 5pm day. Under _____, there is typically a core period of the day when employees are expected to be at work (for example, between 11 am and 3pm), while the rest of the working day is 'flexitime', in which employees can choose when they work, subject to achieving total daily, weekly or monthly hours in the region of what the employer expects, and subject to the necessary work being done.

A _____ policy allows staff to determine when they will work, while a flexplace policy allows staff to determine where they will work.

a. Bennett Amendment
b. Certificate of Incorporation
c. Fiduciary
d. Flextime

29. _____ is a company policy or program that enables employees to have more decision authority on where they will work regardless of time of day. For example, they may choose to work in the office or from home or from a client's office or even a caf>é.

a. 33 Strategies of War
b. 28-hour day
c. Flexplace
d. 1990 Clean Air Act

30. _____, e-commuting, e-work, telework, working from home (WFH), or working at home (WAH) is a work arrangement in which employees enjoy flexibility in working location and hours. In other words, the daily commute to a central place of work is replaced by telecommunication links. Many work from home, while others, occasionally also referred to as nomad workers or web commuters utilize mobile telecommunications technology to work from coffee shops or myriad other locations.

a. Telecommuting
b. 1990 Clean Air Act
c. 33 Strategies of War
d. 28-hour day

31. _____ is a method of supporting unassigned seating in an office environment. It is similar and is sometimes confused with hot desking, another method of supporting unassigned seating. _____ is reservation-based unassigned seating, whereas, hot desking is reservation-less unassigned seating.

a. Hotelling
b. 33 Strategies of War
c. 28-hour day
d. 1990 Clean Air Act

32. A _____ is a form of periodic payment from an employer to an employee, which may be specified in an employment contract. It is contrasted with piece wages, where each job, hour or other unit is paid separately, rather than on a periodic basis.

From the point of a view of running a business, _____ can also be viewed as the cost of acquiring human resources for running operations, and is then termed personnel expense or _____ expense.

a. Salary
b. Human resources
c. Human resource management
d. Training and development

33. A _____ is a compensation, usually financial, received by a worker in exchange for their labor.

Compensation in terms of _____s is given to worker and compensation in terms of salary is given to employees. Compensation is a monetary benefits given to employees in returns of the services provided by them.

Chapter 15. Leading the Growing Company and Planning for Management Succession

a. Performance-related pay
c. Profit-sharing agreement
b. State Compensation Insurance Fund
d. Wage

34. In finance, an _____ is a contract between a buyer and a seller that gives the buyer the right--but not the obligation--to buy or to sell a particular asset (the underlying asset) at a later day at an agreed price. In return for granting the _____, the seller collects a payment (the premium) from the buyer. A call _____ gives the buyer the right to buy the underlying asset; a put _____ gives the buyer of the _____ the right to sell the underlying asset.
   a. A Stake in the Outcome
   c. AAAI
   b. Option
   d. A4e

35. _____ is the state or fact of exclusive rights and control over property, which may be an object, land/real estate or intellectual property. An _____ right is also referred to as title. The concept of _____ has existed for thousands of years and in all cultures.
   a. A Stake in the Outcome
   c. Emanation of the state
   b. A4e
   d. Ownership

36. _____, commonly abbreviated to Gen X, is a term used to refer to a generational cohort of children born after the baby boom ended and usually prior to the 1980s

The term _____ has been used in demography, the social sciences, and marketing, though it is most often used in popular culture.

In the U.S. _____ was originally referred to as the 'baby bust' generation because of the drop in the birth rate following the baby boom.

   a. Abraham Harold Maslow
   c. Affiliation
   b. Generation X
   d. Adam Smith

37. _____ is the process of disassembly and recovery at the module level and, eventually, at the component level. It requires the repair or replacement of worn out or obsolete components and modules. Parts subject to degradation affecting the performance or the expected life of the whole are replaced.
   a. Methods-time measurement
   c. Capacity planning
   b. Productivity
   d. Remanufacturing

38. Feedback describes the situation when output from (or information about the result of) an event or phenomenon in the past will influence the same event/phenomenon in the present or future. When an event is part of a chain of cause-and-effect that forms a circuit or loop, then the event is said to 'feed back' into itself.

Feedback is also a synonym for:

- Feedback signal; the information about the initial event that is the basis for subsequent modification of the event.
- _____; the causal path that leads from the initial generation of the feedback signal to the subsequent modification of the event.

Chapter 15. Leading the Growing Company and Planning for Management Succession

Feedback is a mechanism, process or signal that is looped back to control a system within itself. Such a loop is called a _____.

a. Negative feedback
c. Positive feedback
b. 1990 Clean Air Act
d. Feedback loop

39. _____ is a method by which the job performance of an employee is evaluated _____ is a part of career development.

_____s are regular reviews of employee performance within organizations

Generally, the aims of a _____ are to:

- Give feedback on performance to employees.
- Identify employee training needs.
- Document criteria used to allocate organizational rewards.
- Form a basis for personnel decisions: salary increases, promotions, disciplinary actions, etc.
- Provide the opportunity for organizational diagnosis and development.
- Facilitate communication between employee and administraton
- Validate selection techniques and human resource policies to meet federal Equal Employment Opportunity requirements.

A common approach to assessing performance is to use a numerical or scalar rating system whereby managers are asked to score an individual against a number of objectives/attributes. In some companies, employees receive assessments from their manager, peers, subordinates and customers while also performing a self assessment.

a. Performance appraisal
c. Progressive discipline
b. Human resource management
d. Personnel management

40. The term _____ in logic applies to arguments or statements.

An argument is valid if and only if the truth of its premises entails the truth of its conclusion, it would be self-contradictory to affirm the premises and deny the conclusion. The corresponding conditional of a valid argument is a logical truth and the negation of its corresponding conditional is a contradiction.

a. 1990 Clean Air Act
c. Simplification
b. Fuzzy logic
d. Validity

41. In human resources or industrial/organizational psychology, _____,' 'multisource feedback,' or 'multisource assessment,' is feedback that comes from all around an employee. '360' refers to the 360 degrees in a circle, with an individual figuratively in the center of the circle. Feedback is provided by subordinates, peers, and supervisors.

a. Job knowledge
c. 360-degree feedback
b. Personnel management
d. Revolving door syndrome

Chapter 15. Leading the Growing Company and Planning for Management Succession

42. _____ is the process of subjecting an author's scholarly work, research, or ideas to the scrutiny of others who are experts in the same field. _____ requires a community of experts in a given field, who are qualified and able to perform impartial review. Impartial review, especially of work in less narrowly defined or inter-disciplinary fields, may be difficult to accomplish; and the significance of an idea may never be widely appreciated among its contemporaries.

   a. 28-hour day
   b. 1990 Clean Air Act
   c. 33 Strategies of War
   d. Peer review

43. In business and accounting, _____s are everything of value that is owned by a person or company. Any property or object of value that one possesses, usually considered as applicable to the payment of one's debts is considered an _____. Simplistically stated, _____s are things of value that can be readily converted into cash.

   a. A Stake in the Outcome
   b. AAAI
   c. Asset
   d. A4e

44. A _____ is typically created as part of an A/B Living trust estate plan after the death of the first spouse to die. During life, a married couple transfers ownership of property into a trust. Upon the death of the first party to die, the terms of the trust require that some portion of the property be transferred into 'TRUST A' and some other portion into 'TRUST B.' The first of these trusts, A, holds property that remains accessible to the surviving spouse during his or her life.

   a. 1990 Clean Air Act
   b. 28-hour day
   c. Joint and several liability
   d. Bypass trust

45. _____ is the process of disposing of an estate. _____ typically attempts to eliminate uncertainties over the administration of a probate and maximize the value of the estate by reducing taxes and other expenses. Guardians are often designated for minor children and beneficiaries in incapacity.

   a. A4e
   b. AAAI
   c. Estate planning
   d. A Stake in the Outcome

46. A _____ is a form of partnership similar to a general partnership, except that in addition to one or more general partners (GPs), there are one or more limited partners (_____s.) It is a partnership in which only one partner is required to be a general partner.

   The GPs are, in all major respects, in the same legal position as partners in a conventional firm, i.e. they have management control, share the right to use partnership property, share the profits of the firm in predefined proportions, and have joint and several liability for the debts of the partnership.

   a. Private equity
   b. Pension fund
   c. Growth capital
   d. Limited partnership

47. A _____ is a formal statement of a set of business goals, the reasons why they are believed attainable, and the plan for reaching those goals. It may also contain background information about the organization or team attempting to reach those goals.

   The business goals may be defined for for-profit or for non-profit organizations.

   a. Business plan
   b. Time management
   c. Distributed management
   d. Crisis management

Chapter 15. Leading the Growing Company and Planning for Management Succession

48. A _____ is a documented investigation of a Market that is used to inform a firm's planning activities particularly around decision of: inventory, purchase, work force expansion/contraction, facility expansion, purchases of capital equipment, promotional activities, and many other aspects of a company.

Not all managers are asked to conduct a _____, but all managers must make decisions using _____ data and understand how the data was derived. So all managers need a reasonable understanding of the tools most used for making sales forecasts and analyzing markets.

a. 1990 Clean Air Act
b. Market analysis
c. Marketing research
d. Marketing research process

49. _____ is an advertisement in which a particular product specifically mentions a competitor by name for the express purpose of showing why the competitor is inferior to the product naming it.

This should not be confused with parody advertisements, where a fictional product is being advertised for the purpose of poking fun at the particular advertisement, nor should it be confused with the use of a coined brand name for the purpose of comparing the product without actually naming an actual competitor. ('Wikipedia tastes better and is less filling than the Encyclopedia Galactica.')

In the 1980s, during what has been referred to as the cola wars, soft-drink manufacturer Pepsi ran a series of advertisements where people, caught on hidden camera, in a blind taste test, chose Pepsi over rival Coca-Cola.

a. 33 Strategies of War
b. 28-hour day
c. Comparative advertising
d. 1990 Clean Air Act

50. A _____ is a group of people or organizations sharing one or more characteristics that cause them to have similar product and/or service needs. A true _____ meets all of the following criteria: it is distinct from other segments (different segments have different needs), it is homogeneous within the segment (exhibits common needs); it responds similarly to a market stimulus, and it can be reached by a market intervention. The term is also used when consumers with identical product and/or service needs are divided up into groups so they can be charged different amounts.

a. Market segment
b. SWOT analysis
c. Customer relationship management
d. Context analysis

51. _____ is one of the four Ps of the marketing mix. The other three aspects are product, promotion, and place. It is also a key variable in microeconomic price allocation theory.

a. Transfer pricing
b. Penetration pricing
c. Pricing
d. Price floor

52. _____ generally refers to a list of all planned expenses and revenues. It is a plan for saving and spending. A _____ is an important concept in microeconomics, which uses a _____ line to illustrate the trade-offs between two or more goods.

a. Budget
b. 1990 Clean Air Act
c. 33 Strategies of War
d. 28-hour day

53. An _____ is any party that makes an investment.

The term has taken on a specific meaning in finance to describe the particular types of people and companies that regularly purchase equity or debt securities for financial gain in exchange for funding an expanding company. Less frequently, the term is applied to parties who purchase real estate, currency, commodity derivatives, personal property, or other assets.

a. A4e
b. A Stake in the Outcome
c. AAAI
d. Investor

Chapter 1
1. d	2. d	3. b	4. c	5. b	6. d	7. b	8. b	9. d	10. d
11. b	12. d	13. c	14. a	15. b	16. d	17. c	18. d	19. d	20. c
21. d	22. c	23. d	24. c	25. a	26. d				

Chapter 2
1. a	2. a	3. d	4. a	5. d	6. a	7. c	8. b	9. c	10. d
11. a	12. d	13. a	14. d						

Chapter 3
1. b	2. d	3. a	4. b	5. d	6. d	7. c	8. c	9. d	10. a
11. c	12. c	13. c	14. b	15. d	16. c	17. b	18. b		

Chapter 4
1. c	2. c	3. a	4. a	5. d	6. b	7. c	8. c	9. c	10. a
11. a	12. b	13. a	14. d	15. c	16. a	17. d	18. c	19. c	20. c
21. b	22. a	23. c	24. b	25. d	26. d	27. d	28. c	29. d	30. a
31. d	32. d	33. d	34. d	35. b					

Chapter 5
1. d	2. d	3. b	4. a	5. d	6. c	7. d	8. c	9. d	10. c
11. a	12. b	13. d	14. d	15. c	16. d	17. d	18. a	19. c	20. b
21. d	22. d	23. d	24. d	25. b					

Chapter 6
1. d	2. d	3. c	4. d	5. d	6. d	7. d	8. d	9. d	10. b
11. d	12. d	13. c	14. b	15. b	16. a	17. d	18. b	19. d	20. a
21. b	22. c	23. a	24. c	25. d	26. c	27. b	28. b	29. c	30. b
31. d	32. d	33. d	34. a	35. c	36. d	37. d	38. d	39. d	40. d
41. a	42. b	43. c	44. d						

Chapter 7
1. b	2. c	3. b	4. a	5. d	6. d	7. d	8. d	9. a	10. a
11. a	12. d	13. d	14. d	15. d	16. d	17. c	18. b	19. a	20. d
21. d									

Chapter 8
1. d	2. d	3. c	4. c	5. a	6. b	7. d	8. d	9. d	10. b
11. d	12. d	13. d	14. d	15. b	16. c	17. d	18. a	19. a	20. c
21. b	22. d	23. d	24. d	25. d	26. c	27. b	28. d	29. d	30. a
31. d	32. d	33. c	34. c	35. c	36. d	37. b	38. b		

Chapter 9
1. a	2. d	3. a	4. d	5. a	6. d	7. d	8. d	9. d	10. d
11. a	12. d	13. b	14. d	15. a	16. a	17. b	18. b	19. d	20. c
21. d	22. a	23. c	24. b	25. d					

ANSWER KEY

Chapter 10
1. d   2. b   3. b   4. c   5. d   6. d   7. d   8. d   9. d   10. d
11. d   12. a   13. c   14. a   15. b   16. b   17. d   18. d   19. d   20. d
21. d   22. c   23. b   24. a   25. d   26. b   27. d   28. a   29. a   30. d
31. b   32. d   33. d   34. b   35. c   36. b   37. d   38. b   39. d   40. b
41. d

Chapter 11
1. d   2. d   3. a   4. a   5. c   6. d   7. d   8. a   9. d   10. b
11. a   12. d   13. a   14. d   15. d   16. c   17. d   18. a   19. d   20. c
21. d   22. d   23. d   24. d   25. d   26. c   27. a   28. b   29. a   30. c
31. b   32. d

Chapter 12
1. d   2. a   3. b   4. d   5. d   6. d   7. a   8. d   9. c   10. d
11. d   12. d   13. b   14. d   15. d   16. a   17. d   18. d   19. c   20. d
21. d   22. b   23. b   24. d   25. d   26. d   27. b   28. d   29. d   30. d
31. d   32. c   33. d   34. d   35. d   36. d

Chapter 13
1. d   2. d   3. a   4. d   5. c   6. b   7. a   8. c   9. d   10. c
11. a   12. b   13. c   14. b   15. a   16. a   17. d   18. a

Chapter 14
1. d   2. d   3. d   4. d   5. d   6. d   7. a   8. d   9. d   10. c
11. d   12. d   13. a   14. b   15. b   16. d   17. d   18. d   19. c   20. d
21. d   22. d   23. d

Chapter 15
1. d   2. d   3. a   4. c   5. c   6. a   7. a   8. c   9. b   10. b
11. c   12. c   13. a   14. b   15. b   16. b   17. c   18. a   19. b   20. c
21. d   22. a   23. b   24. d   25. d   26. d   27. b   28. d   29. c   30. a
31. a   32. a   33. d   34. b   35. d   36. b   37. d   38. d   39. a   40. d
41. c   42. d   43. c   44. d   45. c   46. d   47. a   48. b   49. c   50. a
51. c   52. a   53. d

www.ingramcontent.com/pod-product-compliance
Lightning Source LLC
Chambersburg PA
CBHW081845230426
43669CB00018B/2824